How to be a Successful Form Tutor

**Related titles:**

Adrian Percival and Susan Tranter: *How to Run your School Successfully*

Chris Turner: *How to Run your Department Successfully*

# How to be a Successful Form Tutor

Michael Marland and Rick Rogers

**continuum**
LONDON • NEW YORK

**Continuum International Publishing Group**
The Tower Building                      15 East 26th Street
11 York Road                            New York, NY 10010
London
SE1 7NX

**British Library Cataloguing-in-Publication Data**
A catalogue record for this book is available from the British Library.

ISBN 0 8264 7197 8 (paperback)

**Library of Congress Cataloguing-in-Publication Data**
A catalogue record for this book is available from the Library of
Congress.

Typset at The Spartan Press Ltd,
Lymington, Hants

Printed and bound in Great Britain by CPI Bath.

# Contents

*'A Form Tutor
is a teacher
whose subject is
the pupil herself.'*

# Acknowledgements

We wish to thank the following for their cogent suggestions, for which we have been very grateful (of course, any errors are our responsibility alone):

Susie Campbell, Linda Chaplin, Dr Matthew Hordes, Colleen McGlaughlin, Michelle McGrath, Jane Moses, Ian Storey, Yasue Tatebayashi, and postgraduate students of the University of London's Institute of Education, Master of Teaching degree course.

We are also grateful to the following for permission to include examples of worksheets which they have devised:

Anna Dolezal, p. 53; Linda Marsh, p. 125; Frank Monaghan, p. 61; Chris Watkins pp. 32 & 106; Adam Weinbren, p. 44.

Some parts of this book are derived from the authors' earlier work, *The Art of the Tutor*, published by David Fulton Publishers in 1997.

# 1 The idea of a Form Tutor

## The centrality of the Form Tutor

Pastoral care enables pupils to make best use of all aspects of their schooling to benefit all aspects of themselves – and the form tutor is the heart of that activity. At the heart of the work of a secondary school is enabling a child to become a student and develop fully as a person. Many epitomize this in their statement of aims. For example, one school has this over-arching statement:

> To enable each young person for whom it is responsible to develop her or his own personal, intellectual, moral, physical, aesthetic, and social understanding and skills to the highest possible levels so that he or she is best placed to shape her or his own life and at the same time to develop an understanding and sympathy for others, their ways of life, and their cultures.
>
> (North Westminister Community School, 1991)

This positive entitlement requires the pastoral work of the school. To enable every child to become a student and develop her or himself as a person is the major task of the tutor's charge of being responsible for personal, educational and vocational guidance. Every teacher is working to help the pupils' growth and in most schools there is a Head of Year or Head of House to take middle-management overall responsibility. However, the tutor is the integrative centre for the school's efforts in personal development, from attendance to welfare, study skills to behaviour.

For every secondary pupil there is what the psychologist, Erik H. Erikson, called 'the crisis of identity'. He defined the central adolescent task as answering the question: 'What do I want to make myself and what do I have to work with?' (Erikson, 1971, p. 314). Thus the tutor's key pastoral task is to enable the tutee to develop her or his exploration of those questions in terms ranging from relationships with peers in class to society more generally, and especially encouraging self-understanding.

The tutor's main aim then is to help the tutee decide who she is, how she wants to be, and how she can change her behaviour in whatever aspects she wishes. This is 'personal guidance'.

If the tutee is to be able to achieve this, she or he must be able to make for herself or himself best use of the school – to exploit it, if you like. To be successful, the child has to learn how to be a pupil – a huge and complex learning task. This is the tutor's role of 'educational guidance'.

It is clear that success at school has a range of effects on the young person's 'pathways from childhood to adult life'. Not only does the more frequently discussed examination portfolio open up or close down certain paths, and therefore certain occupations, milieux, and income levels, but success or failure to take a grip on school can influence a person's ability to cope in the future: 'There is evidence that successful coping and/or positive experiences tend to be protective, and it is possible that the protection lies in the enhanced self-confidence that derives from the experiences.' (Rutter, 1989, p. 43)

One of the daunting but also encouraging aspects of responsibility for pastoral care is the research confirmation that success at school positively affects most aspects of later life. This is not only a direct result of examinations, but also of the range of experiences. In the case of institution-reared girls for instance:

> Positive school experiences were associated with an increased tendency to exert 'planning' in relation to both marriage and careers. It is suggested that this was because the successful coping in one situation – school – increased the likelihood that the girls would feel in control of other aspects of their lives and able to do something about the situation.
>
> (Rutter, 1989, pp. 43–4)

Every teacher and every aspect of the environment and procedures of a school should be calculated to offer the possibility of positive, successful coping and the building of appropriate self-esteem. However, this is the tutor's special responsibility: through the tutor's guidance the growing student is better able to make school cohere and find modes of success. If there were no tutors in a school there would be no 'home' for a pupil to go to when he or she needed it. The tutor's offer of 'home' is, though, not a mere soft cushion: at its best a home makes demands, enables growth, stimulates imagination, encourages self-esteem, develops judgement, creates a sense of coherence, and provides security.

A pupil needs to feel safe in the wider community of the school. This, of course, includes the physical, and even petty bullying and racial or sexual harassment are clearly very distressing, having effects well beyond the immediate impact of the incidents themselves. More than that, though, all pupils need to feel psychologically comfortable – able to be themselves without either being totally pulled into the peer group's way or being ostracized. The tutor contributes to meeting this need in two complementary ways: firstly, by the development of the tutee's appropriate assertiveness and inter-personal skills through the group tutorial programme; secondly, by creating in the tutor room and in the tutor group a mutually supportive atmosphere: 'Sir, do you know what happened to Ramesh today?' The tutor should encourage the end-of-the-day bringing back of the pleasures and difficulties of that day. There is ample evidence that in most secondary schools the students report that they are more likely to turn to their tutor: 'Nearly a quarter of the teenagers who could talk to a member of staff about personal relationships said they would turn to their form tutor.' (Allen, 1987)

Bombarded with urgent demands to complete tasks, the tutor can become an overloaded functionary, reeling from problems and rarely in a position to look ahead. Like so many Year Heads, tutors are then forced to be reactive and not proactive. If pastoral care is limited to coping with problems, it will not be possible to meet the major needs of the tutees in the welter of effort to cope with the demands of the daily round.

A tutor's pastoral care can never be successful unless it pulls itself above this responding to what has gone wrong and looks ahead, using the group and group-study material and activities to help the individual understand herself or himself better, and from that develop the more appropriate behaviours. It is also about helping young people look to the future, both immediate and distant, and to take control of their inner, their social and their learning lives.

The tutor must teach the group to make sense of, but be independent of, social and peer-group pressures.

This target of personal-social growth is, obviously, a central aim of the whole-school curriculum, but the tutor is the special exponent. The tutor's narrower, specific responsibilities, such as home-school liaison, welfare support, individual counselling, and discipline, are only parts of the tutorial role and must always be interpreted in the light of the larger task: the sum of the details will not necessarily create the required whole. Busy application to a myriad of tasks can obscure the guidance role. Each needs seeing and meeting in the light of the overall task, and that also needs embodying in specially planned whole-group work.

Difficult as the task of tutoring is, the key to success is to have a firm vision of the *idea* of a tutor and to exploit the tasks to serve this vision.

## The Form Tutor and the task of the school

The way the National Curriculum requirements for the School Curriculum were defined in the fundamental legislation of 1988, and the mechanical interpretation which followed, over-stressed the National Curriculum aspect and under-stressed the pastoral preliminary to the Curriculum section.

Although not sufficiently noticed at the time, there is a real sense in which the late twentieth-century legislation put pastoral care at the heart of schooling. The *Education Reform Act 1988* preceded its introduction of the National Curriculum with a powerful over-arching requirement, which covers all aspects of schooling and is crucial to tutoring. It declared that the curriculum of the school must be a 'balanced and broadly based' one which:

(a) promotes the spiritual, moral, cultural, mental and physical development of pupils at the school and of society; and

(b) prepares such pupils for the opportunities, responsibilities and experiences of adult life

*(Education Reform Act 1988*, section 1 (2))

In the early years of the twenty-first century, a small, but significant change in the wording of the last phrase appropriately highlighted the pastoral role of enabling the pupil to develop as an effective student in the older years at school and in higher education: 'adult life' was changed in the 2002 legislation to 'later life', which clearly includes schooling and higher education.

The requirement that a school must prepare the pupils for 'the opportunities, responsibilities and experiences of later life' indeed strengthens the idea of the tutor (*Education Act 2002*, section 78 (1)).

The *Children Act 1989* and the *Education Act 1993* further heightened the rights of children:

- the child's welfare is paramount and safeguarding and promoting it is the priority
- local authorities have a duty to ensure that support services for children 'in need' are provided and should minimise unnecessary intrusion into family life
- service providers must listen to and work in partnership with children, parents, any who have parental responsibility, and relevant others

The 1993 legislation was particularly important in that it gave legal force to the need to listen to children and developed and defined Special Educational Needs very precisely and ambitiously.

Towards the end of the 1990s, there was a freshly stressed emphasis on pupils' spiritual and moral development. An important 1996 SCAA (School Curriculum and Assessment Authority) conference summed up 'What schools could be doing':

There was general agreement that schools should seek to be explicit and coherent about the values that guide their practice. Teachers should actively plan the best way to communicate these values in the classroom. There should be parity between the ideals expressed in a school prospectus and the reality a pupil experiences within the school community. Consciously or not, all teachers convey the virtues they most value and how these virtues can be put into practice. This perhaps underlines the need for some common agreement on values.

The conference felt strongly that schools needed to develop the skills that enable young people to make wise decisions and develop acceptable values, attitudes and behaviour. These should not take second place to skills that are more readily assessed. A number of delegates expressed the view that we place too much emphasis on preparation for work and not enough on preparation for life, particularly self-development in terms of spiritual, physical, sexual, social, vocational and moral attributes and qualities. A practical recommendation was that any list of 'key skills' should include 'skills for life'.

(SCAA, 1996, p. 11)

While there was and will continue to be arguments about how to define values in our pluralistic society, it is clear schools have this kind of responsibility as a fundamental aim, which is logically prior and hierarchically superior to the National Curriculum's minimum content specifications.

## Personal and social development

Most schools have a whole-school curriculum plan for 'personal and social development', and this is most effective if it weaves into most of the subject courses as well as having a specific PSHE or Citizenship timetabled course. However, the tutor has a key role in this whole-school approach. For instance, the tutor will often be reviewing and exploring problems faced by members of his or her tutor group. The temptation is to rush to give terse advisory 'instruction'. Often, though, this is an occasion for a tutorial exploration of 'problem solving', bringing the generalities to bear on the particular issues your tutees are facing. The Gulbenkian Foundation's study of personal and social development sums up the overall challenge, which is a key part of the tutor's role:

Everyday problem-solving is a process that entails clarifying the problem, generating different solutions through brainstorming, evaluating and selecting the best solution. Pupils need to be aware of different ways to make decisions and the skills that are essential to the process.

(Lees and Plant, 2000, p. 39)

The tutor has a very central role in a whole-school 'personal and social' development approach, even when these are specialist PSE/PSHE/Citizenship teachers with subject-course periods time-tabled. Again, as the Gulbenkian study points out:

> Tutors often have a good relationship with their forms: they know the pupils well and can help them to review their personal and social development and set personal goals. Tutor groups frequently have responsibility for organising school events, such as assemblies, which provide excellent opportunities for the pupils to develop and demonstrate their skills and confidence.
>
> (*op. cit.*, p. 36)

All aspects of the work of the school have a pastoral dimension: the courses, the communal activities, beyond-timetable voluntary activities, residential experiences, and any 'timetable overlays' or special events. There may well be specific courses on aspects of spiritual, social and moral development, e.g. short courses on sexuality, careers, assertiveness, to give actual examples from particular schools. Most schools have a continuous 'PSHE' and a Citizenship course delivered by specialists. However, in all these patterns the work of the tutor brings together the pastoral curriculum, and brings the personal, vocational and social guidance of the individual in all aspects of the school together so that the tutees can see the relationships between the aspects. The tutor is thus 'the integrative centre' for the school's whole curriculum.

## The group and the individual

Later we devote a chapter both to *Managing the Tutorial Sessions* and *Individual Casework*: both are important. There appears at first to be a tension between them. Indeed a fundamental pedagogical difficulty grows out of the central aim of pastoral care: if it is about helping the individual understand herself, how can the tutor find time and space to work with all these individuals? Tutors often feel a frantic wish to send all but one tutee away.

Despite the national assessment of schools by available statistics, a school's central concern is for developing as far as possible the growth of individuals. Yes, they often share characteristics in common, but in baffling combinations. The school has to plan its curriculum and its procedures in a fairly standard way for all, and most of the time the pupils have to work in fairly large teaching groups.

Thus the art of the pastoral care of the tutor has been defined as 'to help all the individuals without always giving individual help' (Marland, 1980, p. 153). The tutees who are in the group should as individuals be in the forefront of the tutor's ambitions, but it is the *group* that will normally have to be the vehicle for helping those individuals. This is partly for the negative reason that there will never be more than a very small amount of time for each individual, but also for the much more positive reason that the group of people is a good medium for learning about people! The other members are not, as they sometimes appear, in, say, an art or mathematics lesson, 'in the way' between the pupil and the teacher: the other tutees and the individual's reaction to them are part of the learning material. Indeed, a well-mobilized group (as is discussed in Chapter 3) is also part of the teaching: there is a sense in which the tutor's task is to enable the group partly to tutor itself.

Of course, that emphasis on the importance of the tutor group as a whole does not take the place of knowing each pupil very well and monitoring each in a very detailed way. Thus the tutor is also the integrative centre for the pupil and the life of the school. It is the tutor who brings the closest and widest knowledge of the individual pupil and the multifarious activities of the secondary school together as positively as possible.

Chapter 7 sets out many details of the individual casework that this concern for the individual engenders. The tutor will be reviewing not only what he or she sees of the tutees, but also what comes from others in the school, sometimes the slightest flicker of minor information. The tutor then puts these together and gives or seeks additional encouragement for these aspects. Often this will identify strengths needing praise or aptitudes justifying additional help. Often this will also identify difficulties requiring support.

Some pupils will be at or towards the extreme ends of intellectual or behavioural difficulties, so much so that they will need additional, specialized help, often individually and separately from the group, even sometimes in special schools. The early identification of these needs is very important, and was heavily stressed by the first official *Code of Practice*, which derives from the key legislation of 1993, 'all children with special educational needs should be identified and assessed as early as possible and as quickly as is consistent with thoroughness' (DfE, 1994, p. 2).

The 1996 legislation, expounded in the *Code of Practice*, makes it clear that: 'Governing Bodies should, with the head teacher, decide the school's general policy and approach to meeting pupils' special educational needs for those with and without statements. They must set up appropriate staffing and funding arrangements and oversee the school's work' (DfES, 2001a, p. 5). It is required that all schools 'must have a written SEN policy' (*op. cit.*, p. 8), and a specified 'member of staff . . . who has responsibility for co-ordinating SEN provision within that school. In a small school the head teacher or deputy may take that role. In large schools there may be a SEN co-ordinating teams' (*op. cit.*, p. 206).

Within this statutory framework, the tutor has a key role. Indeed, other than those pupils who come to the school already identified and analysed, the tutor has an initial role in sensing the need through a variety of clues and passing this to the Head of Year for further consideration. The Special Educational Needs Coordinator (SENCO) or Head of Year will no doubt wish to consult the tutor for her or his overview. The tutor is not a trained specialist in special educational needs, but is something of a specialist in *this child*.

Indeed, the *Code* gives the tutor a key role in the early stages:

Stage 1 is characterised by the gathering of information and increased differentiation within the child's normal classroom work. At this stage, the child's class teacher or form/year tutor:

- identifies a child's special educational needs
- consults the child's parents and the child
- informs the SEN co-ordinator, who registers the child's special educational needs
- collects relevant information about the child, consulting the SEN co-ordinator

- works closely with the child in the normal classroom context
- monitors and reviews the child's progress

(DfEE, 1994, pp. 21–2)

While the precise division of responsibilities will vary from school to school, the centrality of the tutor's care for the individual is well demonstrated by these key SEN duties.

Demanding as it is, this interest in and care for the individual is the key to the idea of the secondary tutor – and very personally and professionally rewarding.

## The difficulties of tutoring

A teacher brings to the pupils a range of skills, knowledge, understanding of concepts, and attitudes. Some of these have been systematically learned and the teacher's grasp of them is conscious and can be coherently articulated. Thus, a science teacher's scientific knowledge and a French teacher's understanding of the French language are the result of clearly focused study. However, other aspects of a teacher's abilities have for years in the past been far less precisely defined or consciously learned. They are far less coherently expressible: our way of analysing problems, our views on the use of time, our 'teaching' about ways of relating to each other – these, and many more aspects of our teaching, are erratic, intangible, and less available for scrutiny, and thus criticism or support. The central reason why tutoring is difficult is that the tutor's main contributions are culled from those less-defined aspects of a teacher's professional concerns.

Of the pastoral specialism, the tutor usually brings little systematic background study and little more specific knowledge than that potentially possessed by the pupil. This removing of a strong expertise, such as the physical education teacher or the history teacher has, can sometimes lead to the tutor feeling lost.

A further difficulty is an iatrogenic one – that is a disease caused by the doctors themselves! Although many schools speak of the importance of tutoring, and some heads speak of the tutor as 'the heart of the school', many schools find it difficult to make the physical and organizational support of tutoring easy. The impact of the National Curriculum aspects of education legislation initially deprived the tutorial role of its necessary emphasis in some parts of the secondary schooling system.

Thus in some schools:

- the requirement of being a tutor is not included in the advertisements
- similarly, it is sometimes not in the job specification
- frequently it is not covered in the interview
- there is sometimes a poor or non-existent job description
- there is little opportunity to be briefed by the team leader
- there are few or no team meetings
- material for tutorial sessions is skimpy – or there may be none
- tutorial material storage is inadequate
- there are inadequate clerical, reception and communication facilities
- there is too little time for tutorial work

Indeed, more generally, pastoral care is undervalued in some schools. In well-run schools middle-management pastoral team-leaders will give detailed briefings and help by observing tutor period sessions, swapping good ideas, and giving detailed observation notes. There will be clear policy and procedure descriptions. There should be planning and discussion meetings for tutors under the leadership of these team leaders, which are also excellent times to pick up tips from others so that each member of the team pools her or his problems and successes and gains from other team members.

## Training

Traditionally the form tutor's role has been considerably less well prepared for in training. In the early eighties a study of new teachers in schools showed that this aspect of initial training tailed dismally behind most others investigated. For instance, whereas only some 21 per cent felt less than well prepared for classroom management, the highest figure, 54 per cent, felt themselves 'not well prepared to undertake pastoral duties' (HMI, 1982). A little later the National Association for Pastoral Care in Education surveyed a large sample of teachers working in schools, and found that as many as 87 per cent 'argued that their initial training contained either a negligible amount of work on pastoral care or nothing at all' (Maher and Best, 1984).

Towards the end of the 1980s a report by the then government inspectors was as worrying:

> In only a small proportion of subject method courses were students being given a clear understanding of their role in relation to personal and social development, and in two-thirds of cases this aspect was not actually being covered. Occasionally, a correlation between subject method and education studies offered good opportunities for some discussions of personal and social development.
>
> (HMI, 1987, p. 120)

Thus, for years a huge proportion of teachers had perceived themselves as having inadequate preparation for pastoral care. Essentially we had a profession little trained for its central daily tutorial task, and thus not well placed to help newcomers.

By the late 1990s there were some signs of more specific, extensive and vigorous training, and the Teacher Training Agency required this role to be covered in its demands that teachers should be trained to: 'Contribute to the pupils' wider educational development, including their spiritual, moral, personal, social and cultural development' (Teacher Training Agency, 1997, p. 8).

However, in considering the idea of the tutor it is helpful to remember that the UK education system has always spoken of the importance of the role, but less often defined it or prepared teachers for it. It is easier to face the task if we accept the huge gaps in preparation that we all have.

Sadly, there is virtually no specific description of the pastoral role of the tutor in the 'Professional Standards for Qualified Teacher Status'. It is true that the central requirements for QTS have now required since September 2003 all teachers to have qualities, which meet 'the wider professional demands of being a teacher', and certainly these are especially relevant to the role of the tutor. For instance, the 'Professional Values and Practice' include:

1.1 They have high expectations of all pupils; respect their social, cultural, linguistic, religious and ethnic backgrounds; and are committed to raising their educational achievement.

1.2 They treat pupils consistently, with respect and consideration, and are concerned for their development as learners.

1.3 They demonstrate and promote the positive values, attitudes and behaviour that they expect from their pupils.

1.4 They can communicate sensitively and effectively with parents and carers, recognising their roles in pupils' learning, and their rights, responsibilities and interest in this.

1.5 They can contribute to, and share responsibility in, the corporate life of schools.

1.6 They understand the contribution that support staff and other professionals make to teaching and learning.

The 'Knowledge and Understanding' significantly includes:

2.2 . . . As relevant to the age range they are trained to teach, they are familiar with the Programme of Study for Citizenship and the National Curriculum Framework for Personal, Social and Health Education.

2.4 They understand how pupils' learning can be affected by their physical, intellectual, linguistic, social, cultural and emotional development.

'Monitoring and Assessment':

3.2.4 They identify and support more able pupils, those who are working below age-related expectations, those who are failing to achieve their potential in learning, and those who experience behavioural, emotional and social difficulties.

3.2.7 They are able to use records as a basis for reporting on pupils' attainment and progress orally and in writing, concisely, informatively and accurately for parents, carers, other professional and pupils.

and of 'Teaching and Class Management':

> 3.3.6 They take account of the varying interests, experiences and achievements of boys and girls, and pupils from different cultural and ethnic groups, to help pupils make good progress.

(TTA, 2003a, pp. 3–7)

Although, of course, all subject-course teaching also requires these examples of knowledge, values and skills, the pastoral role of the tutor features these intensely and continuously. Further, they are always developable to a higher level throughout one's career. Tutors who have been given Qualified Teacher Status at the end of their first year of teaching have clearly 'demonstrated' that they have these skills and approaches. However, you will enjoy your role as tutor more and support your pupils even more effectively the further you enrich your depth and skill in these attributes.

## Job description

Most schools do have specific 'job descriptions' for tutors, though these sometimes list the 'tasks' without attempting to define the core of the responsibility for the whole of the pupil's development in school: personal, social, intellectual and cultural.

We recommend tutors to study any job description carefully, ensure each task is carefully carried out, but also ensure that they are woven together within the spirit of enabling the pupil to develop overall. Here is one school's careful and thoughtful approach:

North Westminster Community School: Job Description

Post Title: Form Tutor

Reporting to: House Year Head
Line Management by: House Year Head

Functional Relationships: Teaching staff, office staff, EWO, DH

Purpose of the post
To co-ordinate the learning experiences of every individual
student in their tutor group, in order to promote student
achievement, including well-being.

The Role
The role of the tutor is crucial to the success of the pastoral
system and requires a high level of communicational and organ-
isational skills. Duty of care is a responsibility, which cannot be
separated from the role.

To work under the direction of the House Year Head.
Support policies and procedures that relate to the management
of their tutor group.
Carry out Duty of Care, including be alert to child protection
issues.
Manage the Attendance and punctuality of the Tutor Group.
In collaboration with HYH, and other colleagues, support in
the co-ordination and encouragement of student achievement.
To build and maintain positive parental links.

General Responsibilities

- Support the school's policies and procedures in order to
  achieve the desired outcomes
- To support the Headteacher and the site managers in
  securing an atmosphere and ethos within the school
  which is both learning-orientated and supportive to students, parents and staff
- To fulfil the professional responsibilities outlined in the
  generic job descriptions for subject teachers

Specific Responsibilities
To support student achievement by:

- Academic tutoring
- Communications with staff, parents, and other outside
  agencies
- Co-ordinating the work of the academic and PSHE

tutors, which relates to the achievement of members of the tutor group
- Support in managing transition at all key stages (transfer and induction)
- Identify, set and review targets
- Co-ordinate reports and give feedback to students and their parents

To manage Attendance and Punctuality

- Comply with the legal requirement of marking the register (including use of Bromcom)
- Collecting and distributing of absence notes and any other communications written or otherwise relating to attendance and punctuality
- Celebrate attendance by rewarding students with stickers, certificates, letters home and the use of assemblies
- Active in giving guidance and strategies for attendance and punctuality
- Regular communications with HYH, Attendance Officer, Parents and staff, in order to promote good attendance and punctuality
- Manage and maintain good attendance by regular and active use of attendance data
- Being actively involved in supporting the late detention system

To support school policies by monitoring:

- Homework Diaries
- Targeted weekly reports
- Feedback from staff
- Checking uniform
- Equipment
- Giving important information (internal and external)

To promote the right type of school ethos by:

- Supporting Assertive Discipline

- Working in line with school policies
- Working fairly with all members of the tutor group
- Duty of Care
- Requiring the highest standards in students' behaviour and approach to their work
- Involvement and supporting the work of the student forum

N.B. Job descriptions will be reviewed and re-negotiated from time to time to meet the changing needs of the school.

## Conclusion

Very many teachers find the tutorial aspect of their professional work very rewarding indeed, and are patently successful despite the difficulties. Very many tutees speak warmly and gratefully of the support, encouragement, and demands of their tutors.

The rich diversity of a secondary school deliberately and properly brings each pupil into a learning relationship with a number of specialist teachers and a slighter relationship in corridor and playground with many more. This, of course, contrasts with the primary school pattern, where the one teacher looks after the class for most of the week, with important but limited contributions from specialist teachers. The secondary pupil to be successful has to bring the range of experiences together into a coherent pattern – enabling this is the tutorial role. Thus, the tutor group and the Tutorial Sessions become what we call 'the integrative centre' for the pupil's personal, moral, social, cultural and intellectual growth.

The tutor is nearest to, most often with, and has the widest knowledge of his tutees and should have the closest relationship with them. (Of course, there will be tutees who 'get on better' with other colleagues, but the tutor–tutee relationship should be the most reliable.) This knowing of tutees and having a close relationship with them is necessary but not sufficient. Be wary of those who say the tutor's task is 'getting to know his pupils'. That is a means and not an end. The purpose of that knowledge is to help the tutee help himself be a better student.

Thus, the tutor is the heart of the school, the specialist whose specialism is bringing everything together, whose subject is the pupil herself, who struggles for the tutee's entitlement, and who enables the pupil to make the best use of the school and develop her person. The tutor will be successful to the extent that he keeps this central vision in mind and builds out of it an overarching pattern to which all the details relate.

# 2 Personal–social growth

## Introduction

Pastoral care and the work of the tutor essentially focus on personal development. In this work of personal guidance and enabling the young person to face that question 'Who am I?', what do we mean by 'personal development'? Is it just a warmly meant but vague notion that pupils will develop differently and so this varied development is indeed 'personal' – particular to that person?

If that were to be so, the claim that the tutor is the heart of the school would be a weak one as the tutor would be no more than a facilitator. The phrase means rather: *the further and enhanced development of the tutee as a person.* That is, the tutor's concern with personal development is so called because it is the very quality of 'person' that the tutor seeks to help the tutee develop.

One key process in that development is to help tutees achieve 'rational autonomy'. This clearly means that the tutor cannot merely rely on exhortation and admonition to develop behaviour, because they largely produce only short-term changes in behaviour. Further, the pupil's responses are shaped by extrinsic reasons. The aim of rational autonomy includes knowledge of self, knowledge of others, and knowledge of outcomes. It is also going to emphasize how to develop decision-making skills. Group tutorial work seeks to facilitate that route to rational autonomy.

That is why we started with our definition: 'A Form Tutor is a teacher whose subject is the pupil herself.' The task of the tutor is to enable the pupil gradually but consistently, and through that learning of self, to learn better how to understand others, relate to them, to make good use of the school, and gradually to prepare to take a full place in wider society. The tutor empowers the tutee.

## The idea of a person

What, though, do we mean by 'the qualities of a person', and is a tutor going to have time to lift himself above the business of the administrative chores to consider them, and teach them? Can a tutor have an overview of the aspects of the personal?

We have all become aware of the pejorative meaning of the phrase 'the hidden curriculum', but we are less clear about why we disapprove and what is the alternative. The objection is that no part of the curriculum should be 'hidden', for only if openly defined can the curriculum be debated and agreed (for instance, by parents and governors) and only then consciously built into programmes. Thus many schools have developed 'behaviour codes', which are virtually a curriculum statement.

In some schools the qualities being aimed at are taken for granted and even the most major ones are left to the tutee's own guess. A few get declaimed from the assembly platform, and many schools have developed a systematic description of such aims.

In planning the growth of tutees up the years of a tutorial programme, it is necessary to have some analytical framework for our concept of the 'the personal'. What aspects of 'a person' are we concerned with?

One sevenfold set of distinctions that draws upon common-sense terminology was drawn up by Richard Pring, and we regard it as a really useful analysis for the new century:

1. Intellectual virtues
   (Those skills and abilities of the mind that allow accurate observation, clear thought, hypothesis, logical argument, and expositions.)
2. Moral virtues
   ('Dispositions such as modesty, kindness, patience, generosity, which govern the emotions.')
3. Character traits
   ('Those qualities of the "will" such as perseverance or courage which are separate from (2) and can be a bad thing if linked with a lack of intellectual or moral virtues.')
4. Social competencies
   (That is, the skills such as oral, bodily, dressing, under-

standing situations, and handling organisations, which are required to make the first three operational: a person can be intellectually vigorous, morally fine, and generously disposed but sadly incompetent to make anything of those qualities.)

5. Practical knowledge
   (Which is necessary also for (4) to operate.)
6. Theoretical knowledge
   (The 'concepts, beliefs, principles, insights afforded through theoretical study'.)
7. Personal values
   (These are not synonymous with (2) and (3): 'Two people could be equally gentle and considerate but disagree on the value of pacifism.')

(Pring, 1984, pp. 22–4)

Such a model of attitudes, concepts and skills required to make each of us a person must underlie the programme of tutorial work. The pastoral curriculum should look to all seven, and the tutorial team has to find the ways of helping each individual assess his or her own sense of each.

What makes a tutee a developing person is the interaction of each of the seven aspects. The school as a whole will seek to develop all of them, but the tutor will help make the pupil conscious of them and better able to assess and develop them in the social context. In a number of schools these aspects of the curriculum are specifically taught in PSHE, but the tutor has the central task of relating this important aspect of the whole-school curriculum to the actual lives of his or her tutees.

Thus 'personal development' is not just 'developing personally' but developing the person – and that is the core of pastoral care, which every aspect of the work of the tutor must serve. Lord Puttnam stressed the wider and higher ambitions of tutorial periods when he said: 'Delight, wonder, mystery, pity, beauty, and pain are to us as important to our understanding of the human experience as anything I could ever be tested on.'

## Reciprocity

However, 'social' development is an inherent part of 'personal' development, and this is not only to protect the rights of others, but, also because one's view of oneself is deeply affected both by one's view of others and by one's perception of their view of oneself. One cannot understand oneself without understanding others. A pupil's view of his ethnicity or gender, for instance, substantially results from his view of others and thus mutuality is a strong thread of tutorial work. The tutorial task thus involves both the skills of relating to others and also the analysis of one's attitude to other people and its relationship with attitude to self. This reciprocity is important.

It is worth remembering that human beings do not always recognize others as 'persons'. Slaves, black people, those with disabilities, women, for instance, have been put aside at various times in different societies as lacking the full range of human attributes. Such extreme examples should not blind us to the ease with which we write off certain people and occupations as similarly lacking: our tutees share with us the human tendency to refuse to admit the full humanity of some others.

Those who behave least well in their secondary years are usually those who failed to learn to understand themselves and others in infanthood. Extensive research has shown the strong correlation between the early infant years and later school behaviour (e.g. Cohn, 1990). For instance, it is an over-simplification to consider prejudice, especially in terms of racism, as if the issue were only one of a person's view of *others*. Few aspects of tutoring reveal the reciprocity of personal development so clearly: view of self and view of others are deeply related.

Sir Peter Newsam, when he was Chairman of the Commission for Racial Equality, put the paradox very clearly. He described racial prejudice as being less the result of our view of the inferiority of others than our view of ourselves:

> Racial discrimination does not proceed, on this theory, from any sense of the inferiority of others. It begins from a particular picture of oneself and the group of which one is part. Other groups, other races, may be held to be as intrinsically to be

valued as ourselves. That is not the problem with their presence. The prejudice against them derives from their inability to become us and the necessity, on this theory, for us to remain as we are or, in some way, perish . . .

It starts – as it did in grotesque form with Hitler – with an exaggerated and inflexible opinion of oneself. So the world is divided into us and not-us; and any threat to us, through too much influence being given to not-us, means that we come to see not-us as the enemy: a presence ultimately hostile to our security.

(Newsam, 1986, pp. 9–10)

No school course which asks young people to address only their views of others will be sufficient: tutoring must ask them to recip-rocate by addressing their view of themselves and, conversely, their view of themselves will affect and be affected by their view of others.

Thus the tutors' task of helping their tutees to sense the 'person' in everyone has two purposes – to help them understand them-selves and to help them relate to others and work successfully with them. This reciprocity is central and the group itself can be de-veloped as a 'laboratory' resource for it: reciprocity with others is partly learned via the activities, conventions and requirements of tutor-group life. The larger aims and the daily details come together with the tutor's blending.

## Knowing and judging

Our profession is properly heavily concerned with cognitive growth and our curriculum is so shaped. Substantially, of course, that is as it should be, but not completely. The tutorial role must include that but go well beyond it to an emphasis on attitudes, morality, respect, skills, and judgement required for decision-making. Many studies in aspects of health education have shown that knowledge is necessary but not sufficient. For instance, a large-scale US study of approaches to changing cigarette-smoking behaviour reported:

Adolescents, therefore, need to be equipped with skills that will permit them to express their own desires and beliefs. Since the peer group is essential to the adolescent's life-style, it is imperative that adolescents learn how to express themselves, follow their own convictions . . . and yet not alienate themselves from their peer group.

(Del Greco, 1980, p. 81)

This, and similar studies, found that 'facts about' were inadequate: a 'life-skills approach' better enabled the student to develop her decision-making confidence.

Writing for the American Health Foundation, Gilbert Botvin summed up the balance, stressing that, while US knowledge-based programmes succeeded in changing students' attitudes about cigarette smoking, they had little impact on actual smoking behaviour: 'Apparently, knowledge of the dangers of cigarette smoking in itself is not a deterrent for most students' (Botvin et al., 1980, p. 140). His New York study of middle and older teenagers concluded that 'any increases in smoking knowledge played only a minor role in reducing the incidence of new smoking'.

Success in enabling young people to change their actions and not just alter their knowledge related to wider approaches to decision-making:

The problem of cigarette smoking was addressed indirectly within the larger context of basic life skills. Included were sessions on self-image, decision-making, advertising techniques, coping with anxiety, communication skills, social skills, and assertiveness training.

(Botvin et al., 1980, p. 137)

In other words, our pupils need knowledge; but for them to alter their actions and styles and to take hold of themselves, facts and intellectual understanding are necessary but not sufficient. As one researcher found: 'At the core of Health Education is informed decision-making' (Balding, 1987, p. 179).

Thus 'personal growth' requires facts but cannot depend on them alone: growth into rational autonomy requires the ability to judge, to enquire, to reject, to be alone without being lonely, and to be able to decide wisely. As Button succinctly puts it: 'It is not enough to know, much less to be told' (Button, 1987, p. 133).

# Cultural, ethnic, and linguistic range

The importance of 'inclusion' and ensuring that pupils of minority ethnic background do not suffer in any way, personal or academic, from any form of racism has been strongly urged on schools. Considerable advances have been made, but in some schools the actual 'anti-racist policy' is focused too narrowly on the deeply important avoiding of racism, but not including the wider pastoral task of understanding one's own and others' ethnic heritage. An important pastoral challenge is the preparation of pupils for a world in which ethnicity and cultural variety are recognized as one of the important aspects of life, and for our pupils we need not only to ensure that none of them suffers as a result of their ethnic heritage, but also that all pupils are enabled to appreciate diversity. The tutor's way of relating to his or her tutees, their use of language, their references in tutor-group discussions, and their specific support on all matters of inter-relationships and approaches to learning requires sensitivity to ethnic, cultural, and linguistic differences – and recognition of the differences.

Although, of course, a major part of this responsibility requires the whole-school curriculum, each subject course, and the communal life of the school to have an inter-cultural approach, the tutor has a key role: his or her responsibility for individual, personal development – and that must relate to the ethnic background of the pupils. Research into aspects of race in schools (e.g. the major Swann Report of 1985, Committee of Enquiry, *Education for All*) has often been weak on pastoral care. However, the Swann Report was built round the one crucial question:

> Membership of a particular ethnic group is however one of the most important aspects of an individual's identity – in how he or she perceives herself and in how he or she is perceived by others.
>
> (Committee of Enquiry, 1985, p. 3)

Thus tutors should not only ensure that minority ethnic pupils are treated fairly, and not 'placed' according to their ethnicity, but that all pupils appreciate their own ethnicity and respect that of others.

For those of minority ethnic and/or language background here are a few basic and sometimes time-consuming points:

- ensure you pronounce your tutee's name as well as possible, both the 'known as' and the full formal name if they differ
- check the family details in the school file, both geographical and in terms of the reasons for moving
- use correctly the titles and names of the parents and carers, e.g. if these are two adults, are they both biological parents of your tutees? Do they give different last names?
- make special efforts to meet parents and carers as often as possible. You will come to really enjoy these meetings, as well as find them helpful for the pupils
- do these tutees have specialist support staff, e.g. EAL teachers, refugee-student advisers, inclusion workers, etc.? If so, ask those members of staff to brief you and keep each of them in touch
- in tutorial discussion sometimes ask pupils to explain points that are not clear to newly arrived pupils

. . . and so on!

It is important to avoid strongly what we term 'inverse racism': that is in an attempt not to criticize unfairly and, to avoid what could be seen as stereotyping, some teachers avoid necessary advice and criticism, For instance, it appears that Afro-Caribbean boys are often allowed to reach a higher level of misbehaviour before they are reprimanded. This comes from the teachers' determination not to be racist, but actually is unfair on those boys and leads to more of them hitting the serious threshold of bad behaviour – and often therefore exclusion. Somewhat similarly, there have been many schools where well-meaning teachers have not corrected pupils' use of non-standard English or worked on their apparent lack of interest in some aspects of the curriculum. Indeed, an extreme example of inverse racism was a teacher objecting to a professional trio playing Brahms in assembly as 'this is a multi-cultural school'.

Do not let us fall into the common trap that inter-cultural education is only for multi-cultural schools. A pupil's experience in the tutor group should deepen and sensitize his or her appreciation of cultural, ethnic and linguistic differences. The tutor can help pupils avoid the two extremes of on the one hand regarding everyone as 'the same' but on the other seeing differences of heritage as putting people apart. This is a fascinating tutorial challenge.

Schools in Norfolk have shown a strong approach. Less than 2 per cent of the population are from minority ethnic heritage, and the teachers have 'made clear their concerns about the difficulties of introducing multicultural themes where there is no local multi-cultural environment' (Watts, 2003, p. 15). A 'World Voices' scheme was established and visits were arranged for presentations to be given, mostly by overseas students at the University of East Anglia. The pupils were very interested and described how they saw differences and similarities.

Tutors in mono-ethnic schools need to find ways of including the development of their tutees' ethnic sensibility for later life. As Ofsted said about raising the attainment of minority ethnic pupils at the turn of the century: 'Effective pastoral care is also charac-terised by the reinforcement of positive behaviour and the high-lighting of respect for others' (Ofsted, 1999, p. 25).

The overwhelming majority of people in Britain of minority ethnic heritage 'assert their Britishness'. A recent study in 2004 (from the Office for National Statistics) showed that the overall figures of those with that approach were 75 per cent of Indian, Pakistani and Bangladeshi groups, 80 per cent of black Caribbeans, and 87 per cent of those of mixed race (Haselden, 2004). The theme that needs to be woven into tutorial work is that British commitment and cherishing of ethnic heritage are not in any way incompatible, and indeed enrich each other. The great education-alist Rabindranath Tagore (who founded his school Shantiniketan in India in 1902 and was the major contributor to the planning of Dartington Hall in England in 1926) showed how we can both learn from and celebrate different cultures admiring their individu-ality at the same time as their shared common aspects. He stressed that there is 'One heart to the globe', but also cherished the variations. A key point for tutors was his stress that 'real unity between diverse groups will only be possible if each group fully realises its own individuality and grows to its full stature'. For tutors his theme is strong: 'The problem the world over is not how to become one through removing individual differences, but how to unite through preserving them.' He summed it up in a tutorial maxim: 'Unity in Diversity.' The togetherness of the members of the tutor group is strengthened by the tutor's reference to cultural, religious and national dates, appropriate mentioning of family events, and interests and enthusiasms of members.

In his urging of countries to include new arrivals on the world day of migrants and refugees in 2004 the Pope used the phrase that would be true for all tutors:

'One discovers the common values of every culture, capable of uniting and not dividing.'

## The constraints of others

An emphasis on personal growth can be misunderstood by some, who think this means unbridled individualism, everything for oneself. The opposite is true: the tutor has to help the tutee recognize and respect the rights of others, to grow the moral consciousness involved, and to find ways of relating to others in a variety of contexts.

We are all used to reprimanding pupils who hurt others, shout over others or are verbally rude. We all seek to encourage respect for other pupils and adults. However, the tutor's role is to do more than notice any failures and reprimand. The tutor in the tutor group enables the tutee to understand the constraints of different facets of society, from the playground to the classroom, the corridor to the street. Conventions are analysed, and their rationale and the limits of their rationality explored. The tutor *uses* incidents of behaviour to help self- and social understanding. For instance, the conventional rules of keeping to the left or the right on roads can be explained in ways that are different from those of greeting a stranger.

It is part of personal growth to internalize the modes of working with others, and part of the tutorial task to help the tutee become *consciously* aware of the constraints of society. As one writer puts it: 'The road to autonomy is paved through the stages of constraint and co-operation' (Kutnick, 1987, p. 70).

It is also clear that all our personal choices are constrained by social pressures. When we emphasize the tutor's task of helping tutees 'take control of their own lives', we realize that this will be a power limited by the environment. Social pressures will always be there, though part of the tutorial task is to free the individual from the 'prison of the peer group' (the phrase is Alex Dickinson's) largely through self-awareness, skills training and the building of self-esteem. We think of the two pressures, self and society, as having a reciprocal relationship. There are some occasions when internal pressures are dominant, but even then the effect of society plays a part. There are few moments when we can truly 'be ourselves' without social pressures reaching us, however tenuously, and there are few moments when the power of the environment is so great that the individual is totally impotent.

## Self-assessment

What do young people make of the intermittent and erratic sequence of feedback that is their experience of schooling? And what do we do to help their interpretation: 'The dominant impression of students is that schools are first and foremost places of evaluation, not of learning' (Covington and Beery, 1976). Sensing this, many schools used to try to de-emphasize testing, and hence were nervous about national assessment. Indeed, many teachers used to go further by attempting to produce motivation and positive inclination by optimistic evaluations that were really unjustified by the actual performance.

The turn of the century has given to schools the strange tension that never has assessment been so dominant in schools, yet the purposes and uses of assessment are often very narrow. The prime purpose should be to help the pupil herself, firstly by enabling the teachers to understand more fully that pupil's characteristics, skills and difficulties further to strengthen the teaching of this particular pupil, and secondly to deepen the pupil's self-assessment and understanding.

The tutorial task from one point of view is to help tutees make good use of the range of evaluations they receive and, indeed, even create additional ones. Young people show variable responses to failure feedback, some deteriorating and others rising to the challenge and even improving their performance in the face of reported failure. The US psychologist, Carol Dweck, has concluded from extensive practical research that: 'The variable that consistently predicts response to failure is the child's interpretation of failure – what he thinks caused it and whether he views it as surmountable' (Dweck, 1977, p. 45). She has further shown that encouragement is best achieved not by doses of readily achieved 'success' but by what she calls 'attribution retraining' – that is, helping the pupils see that the negative feedback can be used as a way of analysing what went wrong, and returning to the task with fresh hope. As she puts it:

> Children's responses to failure feedback are guided by the manner in which they interpret that feedback. For different children failure has different postdictive and predictive value. Helpless children often view failure as conveying information about their abilities and as signalling continued failure. Persistent, mastery-orientated children view failure as carrying information about specific aspects of their performance that are modifiable.
>
> (*op. cit.*, p. 48)

How were the pupils led to understand the SATs (Standard Assessment Tasks) in their primary schools? In too many cases they are prepared for such tests with only one purpose: to show themselves at their best. That is only one aspect: even more important is to learn how to *use* the test result for self-understanding and thus movement forward. 'If my score on that test was $x$, what does that mean, and what should I be doing?' The tutor has a special part to play in this analysis.

The group tutorial work includes as one of its aims enabling the tutee to interpret negative feedback as useful and to arm the tutee with strategies for using criticism. Too often we have attempted this only by exhortation: 'You must all try harder.'

The effective tutor uses group work as well as individual discussion to help the tutee to understand what different reactions (for example, both external and internal tests, marks on exercises, comments) mean and how she can make them coherent. Personal growth requires one's understanding of self, but it is not easy to use the range of response teachers offer: the tutor can enable this.

In a sense the Year 11 Progress File: Achievement Planner is the summation of the tutorial task up the years to help the tutee's self-understanding, which is in a way a rolling programme of a continuous record of achievement.

The tutor will establish points for self-evaluative reflection in each year. The Progress File core of negotiated description, self-evaluation, the collection of samples of work, and notes of achievements should not be left to become a desperate final exercise in the fifth year: rather, that is the culmination of such work up the years, indeed starting in the first year.

Some of this work will require an explanation of the school's and each department's grading scheme. Tutors need to give firm, specific tuition on how the school's systems work and what they mean, for example, what is the referencing — internal or external, norm or criterion?

Similarly, external tests need explaining. The useful axiom is that: 'A test tests only what the test tests.' For instance, a Year 9 SAT reading assessment cannot assess all aspects of reading. Tenacity is barely recognized, and sensitivity of personal response hardly. What do such tests tell the pupil? And how can she or he use this information? As the tutee moves up the years, the review sessions mentioned earlier should become longer, more detailed and in a sense more formal. It is very important that the Progress File reviewing is not left as a sudden change of style and purpose towards the conclusion.

Thus self-evaluation can be started by the tutor at a fairly sophisticated level quite early in the secondary school. A pro forma can prompt. Figure 1 is a self-analytic tutorial worksheet for the end of first year in secondary school.

'Self-conscious' is usually a pejorative word in current use, implying 'awkward', 'embarrassed', 'lacking genuineness'. Yet not to be 'conscious of self' is an unhappy situation. The work of the tutorial programme aims to enable the tutee to be valuably more self-conscious in a positive way. Self-assessment can be taught as part of this, and this involves, as does so much of tutoring, making good use of what the school has to offer. The course teachers and the tutor must teach the pupil how to interpret and sensitively *use* all forms of assessment.

One of the things I've done well at recently has been

. . . . . . . . . . . . . . . . . . . . . . . . . . . . . . . . . . . . . . . . . . .

One of the things I've found difficult recently has been

. . . . . . . . . . . . . . . . . . . . . . . . . . . . . . . . . . . . . . . . . . .

One of the things I've enjoyed most recently has been

. . . . . . . . . . . . . . . . . . . . . . . . . . . . . . . . . . . . . . . . . . .

The things I'm doing best in are . . . . . . . . . . . . . . . . . . .

and the reason is . . . . . . . . . . . . . . . . . . . . . . . . . . . . . .

Things I'm not doing well in are . . . . . . . . . . . . . . . . . .

and the reason is . . . . . . . . . . . . . . . . . . . . . . . . . . . . . .

My parents, and/or the adults I live with seemed proud when

. . . . . . . . . . . . . . . . . . . . . . . . . . . . . . . . . . . . . . . . . . .

I was proud when I . . . . . . . . . . . . . . . . . . . . . . . . . . . . .

Figure 1    Self-analytical tutorial worksheet

## Morality and ethics

Despite the oft-reiterated demands by the public and politicians for schools to 'reinforce morals', there had been rather little exploration of moral and ethical education in this country. Perhaps it had been taken for granted. Also many casual and even a few formally qualified commentators confuse moral education with religious education. Further, the introduction of the 'National Curriculum' in the 1988 legislation led to many people seeing the school curriculum as coterminous with the National Curriculum. Actually, logically prior and hierarchically superior to the National Curriculum required 'elements' was the statutory requirement that the *school* curriculum had to be one which 'promotes the spiritual, moral, cultural, mental and physical development of the pupil'.

At the end of the century, the QCA's overall statement of the 'values, aims, and purposes' of the school curriculum and the National Curriculum was stated as including as its second 'aim' the 'moral' development. By August 2002, schools were required to teach 'citizenship' in Key Stages 3 and 4, including that:

Pupils should be taught to think about topical, political, spiritual, moral, social, and cultural issues, problems and events. In 2004

Ofsted produced a very cogent study *Promoting and evaluating pupils spiritual, moral, social and cultural development*, which sums up: 'Moral development is about the building, by pupils, of a framework of moral values which regulates their personal behaviour. It is also about the development of pupils' understanding of a society's shared and agreed values.' (Ofsted, 2004, p. 13)

(DfEE and QCA, 1999a, p. 24)

Thus 'moral' development is now part of the National Curriculum element of the school curriculum. However, it does not mean that moral matters are taught only in a course called 'Citizenship'. Indeed, the *National Curriculum Handbook* clearly states that 'it is for schools to choose how they organise their school curriculum to include the programmes of study for citizenship' (*op. cit.*, p. 6). The whole school is clearly concerned with moral and ethical education in every aspect of the curriculum, the procedures, the regulations, the relationships, and the ethos. However, it is the tutor who articulates and synthesizes this and, above all, brings otherwise random admonition and precept into a deliberately theoretical and disinterested but emphatic consideration.

However, we do not have a strong tradition for the tutor to draw on. There is in many schools an over-emphasis of the reactive over the proactive. Indeed, most school activity that could be thought of as concerned with ethics is mopping up after 'trouble'. The conscientious teacher will often work very hard to make a lesson out of a reprimand, but there is often insufficient time and an awkwardness of placing when broader ethical questions are introduced into bad-behaviour post-mortems.

In the investigation and follow-up to trouble in all walks of life from families to employment, public order to professional disputes, recourse has to be made to principles. 'That is wrong!' usually needs justifying against a code. In schools of a religious foundation this can be, and often is, done by using the behavioural precepts of that religion. All schools refer to 'the school rules', or, as more recently formulated, the 'Behaviour Code'. Secular schools sometimes refer beyond the internal rules or code to widely held expectations of decency or morality: 'Everyone knows it is wrong to . . .'

However, it is less common for there to be an explicit ethical code to which such exhortations or criticisms refer. Still less often is there a *specific* teaching of the building, consideration, and use of an ethical code. Partly this is because of the immense pressure on a school's curriculum from the demands of breadth: we are teaching more concepts, facts and skills than ever before. Partly, though, it comes from the conviction that children learn best in context. The argument goes that children cannot analyse and discuss right and wrong out of the context of an actual situation. This argument judges as ineffective the 'What if . . . ?' hypothetical discussions.

We judge that for many years in the past there had been a fear of the theoretical. Fifty years or so of the development of trying to involve pupils in heuristic practical work in science, talking and writing in English, and designing and making in design and technology may have left too few opportunities for pupils to consider the range of principles that lie behind such activities. There has sometimes been an imbalance in favour of 'doing'. There is also remarkably little attention to the place of biography in many subjects (e.g. Science, DT, Mathematics), and thus opportunities for considering moral and ethical issues in a human context.

This imbalance not only weakens by too drastically thinning 'theory', it also severely restricts the range of examples that the pupil can meet. The curriculum restriction in design technology is curiously analogous to that in moral considerations: because of the insistence of considering what can be directly experienced, the range of artefacts is limited by the tyranny of the workbench: only small-scale and cheap, readily available materials. Thus there is a very limited range of cultural traditions or periods. Similarly in ethical considerations there is little opportunity to consider dilemmas of the wider adult world or even prepare the pupils for some of the less common but nevertheless possible older teenage ethical tensions. It also reduces the likelihood of the young person sensing in her or his current predicaments the same ethical elements as lie at the heart of major adult decisions.

There have been some studies that show the efficacy of specific teaching. For instance, Geoffrey Short tried 'an initiative to promote social justice' with classes of junior-school children. What could be properly called an ethical code on aspects of unfair discrimination on issues of gender, race and social class was taught:

> The study provides evidence consistent with the claim that children between the ages of seven and eleven can learn to

recognise certain manifestations of unfair discrimination against oppressed groups. The data further suggests that children in this age group can learn to recognise such discrimination on the basis of principles acquired in contexts that make no reference to oppressed groups.

(Short and Carrington, 1991, p. 157)

Such learning should not be entirely left to the contextual, still less to the actual occurrence of poor behaviour. The tutor needs to identify issues and prompt group discussion.

Many group exercises will informally be following a pattern in which a dilemma is put to the tutor group and the morality of possible decisions discussed. The material used should include real and fictional examples, from a variety of sources. Education in morality is not, though, primarily education in *what* you should do but *how* you should arrive at your decision.

Thus, frequently in a tutorial programme, actions will be discussed: 'How would you react if . . . ?' 'What do people do when . . . ?' and 'What did she do in that situation?' The tutor will always have difficulty in focusing not so much on the behaviour as on the cause. Yes, these are universal, though even these can be overruled by higher principles, but these need to be arrived at by focusing on principles, not details. Rules are handy guides but not themselves deeply educative. The tutor is always (perhaps lightly and certainly tactfully) leading back to the ideas and ethical principles that underlie rules.

The process of tutoring is empowering the tutee, but with the giving of self-power must go the development of the ability to be sensitive and appropriately generous. Morality and ethics are at the heart of tutoring.

## Sexuality

The tutor's responsibility for referring when appropriate to any aspect of sexuality presents particular difficulties. This is one of the most contentious elements of the curriculum, and is more difficult to handle in the pastoral role of a tutor than, for instance, in the biology section of the science course. Your school has been required since 2002 to have a sex education policy. The *Education*

*Act 2002* clearly states that the Secretary of State's guidance of Section 403 (1)(a) of the *Education Act 1996* applies, which required the governing body to 'make, and keep up-to-date, a separate written statement of their policy with regard to the provision of sex education'. The 2002 Act also specifically states that the 'basic curriculum for every maintained school in England' should include 'in the case of a secondary school, provision for sex education for all registered pupils at the school' (Section 80 (1) (c)).

Many people in schools (governors, parents and staff) continue to be worried about legal controls over sexual orientation. There never was a statutory obligation against teaching about homosexuality in schools, despite the widespread misunderstanding of Section 28 of the *Local Government Act 1986*. This declared only that 'a Local Authority shall not . . . promote the teaching in any maintained school of the acceptability of homosexuality as a pretended family relationship'. The Department of the Environment stated very clearly indeed in 1988:

> Section 28 does not affect the activities of school governors nor of teachers. It will not prevent the objective discussion of homosexuality in the classroom, nor the counselling of pupils concerned about their sexuality.
>
> (Dept. of the Environment, 1988, para. 20)

At the start of the new century, the government's advice was clear and cogent, and especially relevant to tutors:

> Sexual identity and sexual orientation
> It is up to schools to make sure that the needs of all pupils are met in their programmes. Young people, whatever their developing sexuality, need to feel that sex and relationship education is relevant to them and sensitive to their needs.
>
> The Secretary of State for Education and Employment is clear that teachers should be able to deal honestly and sensitively with sexual orientation, answer appropriate questions and offer support. There should be no direct promotion of sexual orientation.
>
> (DfEE, 2000, pp. 12–13)

The Guidance clearly links 'sex' with 'relationship' as does the tutor's role.

Obviously you need to study your school's policy, and look into the specific teaching given in PSHE and Science.

Your references in tutorial sessions or individually could be prompted by:

- a question from a tutee about relationships
- a misuse of sexually offensive language
- a romantic relationship between a pair of older pupils
- a public news story
- an allegation about the wrongdoing of one of your tutees
- a public story in the press and TV which has a sexual component
- a tutorial discussion about aspects of 'growing up' and 'relationships'

The tutor's task is difficult: to be sensitive but clear, non-intrusive but open, specific but not embarrassing, empathetic but not condoning of actual wrongdoing. It is normally wise not to ask personal questions of individual tutees in the group sessions and not to share personal sexual details of your own except on exceptional occasions (e.g. if an event needs discussing and you had an analogous experience, it can be sensitive to make careful reference). Do not forget that some details that occasionally come to light will need referring to your senior line manager (sexual abuse is discussed on pp. 123–6).

## Conclusion

By placing the growth of the child as a student and as a person at the centre of tutoring, the school is fulfilling a central part of its major statutory, overarching aims: it must prepare the 'pupils at the school for the opportunities, responsibilities and experiences of later life', as the key legislation of 2002 rephrases it (*Education Act 2002*).

This is reiterated in the latest guidance from Ofsted on pupils' spiritual, moral, social and cultural (SMSC) development which, says the document:

. . . is crucial for individual pupils and it is crucial for society as a whole. Most teachers would see it as the heart of what education is all about – helping pupils grow and develop as people.

(Ofsted, 2004, p. 3)

Through that concept of personal-social imperative, the tutor can find the criteria against which her priorities can be judged and by which the details of every action can be shaped. It is from this centre that the heart of group activity in tutorial work grows.

One of the pioneers of group tutorial work in this country, Leslie Button, defined it thus:

Developmental group work is a way of helping people in their personal growth and development, in their social skills and in the kind of relationships they establish with other people. Its purpose is to provide individuals with opportunities to relate to others in supportive groups, to try out new social approaches and to experiment in new roles. Care, concern and the development of responsible attitudes are basic to the work.

(Button, 1987, p. 130)

In this process of enabling personal-social growth, the tutor is using the group as a whole, stimulated by issues, data, texts and ideas put before it to help each of its members develop as a person.

Particular events, episodes in the life of the tutor group, and individual anecdotes and enquiries will be sympathetically but disinterestedly discussed. However, the tutor will help the tutees to weave the threads of the range of their lives and their chance experiences into the warp and weft of a fabric that is for each her own and has a coherent strength.

If the tutor is 'a teacher whose subject is the pupil herself' the aim of that 'subject' is the growth of the tutee as a person in the school and in society, and all the ways and actions of the tutor must be congruent with that aim: everything the tutor initiates and is required to do must be shaped to work towards the social and personal development of her or his tutees.

# 3 Managing the tutorial sessions

It's funny how teachers make out the tutorial period's important, but they don't do anything in it!

[secondary-school pupil]

## Introduction

With what can in some schools look like an insubstantial and vague task, and one weighed down by a plethora of minor 'business', and with their minds on the challenge of their day's subject teaching, tutors often do not know what to do with their group other than 'call' the register, chase missing absence notes, and issue reprimands and the occasional praise for helpfulness. The pupil quoted above speaks for many: what is supposed to be going on?

There is, firstly, a tension between individual casework and group work, and, secondly, between the proactive and the reactive. The struggle is to respond sensitively to individual needs: 'Please, Miss, my maths teacher said . . .', while not being dominated by reacting to the reported worries of your tutees or the complaints about them from your colleagues.

As a subject teacher your aims are fairly homogeneous, and even convergent: you know where you are going. However strongly interested you are in each of the pupils as individuals, the prime intention is clearly that the pupil should achieve the curriculum goals of the subject course. The subject curriculum gives strong direction, a series of steps, an established pedagogy and usually, very helpfully, learning material. Thus the management of the class derives from a generally well-understood aim, sequence and method. Conversely, the tutor's 'subject' lies substantially inside each tutee and thus the course of the tutor-group work is likely to be buffeted by what happens to those individuals.

*The art of managing a tutor group is to balance sensitivity to the tutees' daily demands with an overarching sense of direction derived from the basic purpose of personal and social growth and helping the tutees make best use of the school.*

## Working together

We label some thirty pupils as a 'tutor group' but of course being designated to go to the same room does not make those pupils automatically into a working group. One characteristic of a successful tutor group is that it is self-evaluative as well as self-supportive.

The tutor can make the tutor room an analogy for the social relationship being developed. The tutor room is, as it were, the 'laboratory of pastoral care', and the tutees both the scientists and the experimental material. The tutees learn about personal and social development by a variety of modes, of which a key one is the working of the group and the individual place each has within it. In this way, the reception and support of a new pupil is carried out not only to help that pupil but also as a paradigm of the helping of people everywhere. At the same time the full reception of that new pupil involves all the pupils examining themselves, the group and the school: you cannot explain to a newcomer that which you do not understand. Thus everyone gains personal development from the proper reception of a newcomer.

Similarly, if a member of the group is, say, having continuous difficulty with lateness, the group, or members of it, can be asked to discuss this, and the latecomer helped to help herself with group advice and support.

In these ways the tutees are learning 'personal and social development' through thinking about and actively working with each other. This will rarely happen by chance, and in many groups the opposite is the style of the group: groups can be self-destructive. The tutor can facilitate the supportive working together by a combination of approaches:

- the inclusion of the general subject of working as a group in discussion and group activities – for instance, separately from any specific issue, the principles can be explored: to what extent can a group help an individual?
- the planning of a group approach to a particular event such as the leaving of one member of the group, a religious festival, or a family occasion
- looking back on an event and analysing how well the group worked together

Groups' projects can also focus on:

- group activities, for example, the end–of–year party
- other teachers, for example, how to negotiate a changed homework pattern, or how to handle the situation of a teacher who is not successfully controlling the class
- the tutor room, for example, displays
- events in the home lives of members, for example, birthdays or births of sisters or brothers

The tutor should seek constantly to help the members of the group develop as a group by considering and working together.

The activities derive from the pastoral curriculum aim of the tutorial session. In some ways, the obvious approach is the simplest and most effective: compare a full-group tutorial session with a subject and use the same techniques:

- what is the intended learning outcome in terms of under-standing, attitudes, facts and skills?
- what topic could focus that?
- what learning activities could embody it?
- what learning materials would assist?
- what would be the best shape of the session?

In other words, if you are worried, just think about the aim of the next run of tutor sessions in the way that you would in your own subject specialism, and think up ways of getting the pupils working towards the agreed aim by whatever methods you are most happy with. Don't feel too tied by specific learning material.

'Group' sometimes confuses. We have used the word to contrast with the one-to-one counselling by tutors. It indicates that the tutor is working with the entire tutor group, but as in any other part of our timetabled work it does not imply 'whole-class teach-ing' all the time. Tutors will sometimes want to talk to the whole tutor group, but often pupils will be working in small groups and at other times individually.

*The form tutor's range of skills is different in balance and use from that of many subject specialisms, but there is no teacherly activity that ingenious teachers do not already do in their own subjects from time to time. The art of the tutor is helping the individual without always working with the individual, and this working together teaches about self, others and reciprocity if well devised.*

## Administration

'Administration' is often a pejorative word in schools. Tutors describe many of the tasks assigned to them as 'mere administration' and show their dislike by hurrying through them and treating them as depressing chores: issuing letters, checking homework diaries, checking addresses, arranging for medicals . . . and so on. The tutees rapidly pick up this attitude, the chores take over the programme, tutoring becomes a bore, and, most important, opportunities are missed.

One trouble is that this administration appears to come down from 'the hierarchy', 'them', or 'the school', and not relate to the tutees' needs. Indeed, often these tasks appear even worse: they positively come between the tutor and tutee, not merely chores but blocks.

In the past school administration usually involved giving unnecessary clerical tasks to tutors (for example, sorting report slips into pupils' packs or advising families about attendance) or giving only the boring procedural end of task without its more rewarding professional end (for example, checking family addresses and sending circulars, but not having responsibility for relationship with the home). Now, the nationally newly shaped working conditions should ensure that many of the routines are carried out by others.

However, there will always be some routine procedures that tutors have to incorporate. What look like 'mere' administrative tasks (an unhelpful term) should be made educationally significant by being woven into the core of the tutorial programme – thus checking home addresses and telephone numbers is not a chore but part of learning about communal and institutional support and responsibility. Similarly the use of a final brief tutorial of the day for checking the setting and preparation for the evening's homework is part of the learning–skills aspect of group tutoring.

While the expeditious announcement of, say, medicals should not be a cue for a lecture on preventive medicine, each of the necessary tasks can be adroitly set in the context of 'why?', and related to the overarching tutorial aims of personal and social growth. For instance, the tutors of one part of a school were required to arrange for their groups to elect a representative for the school council, a pupil consultative organization. A tutor could simply announce it as an afterthought, perfunctorily ask for suggestions, and then vote by show of hands – 'Business over, thank heavens!'

Contrasted with that 'chores' approach, one of us observed a two-session approach with a first-year group, in the first of which the tutor reminded the groups that in many walks of life, such as clubs and organizations, especially in our government, representatives are elected. 'Represent' – 'to present' or give, 're-' again. If this group were to be 'represented' by one member to speak for all at meetings, what qualities should that person have?

To help the tutees consider what they wanted from *their* representative, the tutor devised a worksheet (Figure 2) with a choice of approaches a representative might have. Some could be easily dismissed as silly. Others, like consulting the head of textiles over the issue of school ties had a seductive but a spurious attraction. There were then a pair that needed careful thought. The tutees discussed their choice in small groups, and at the end the tutor pooled their arguments. Only in the *next* tutorial session did the nominating and voting start. Thus the tutor seized a school administrative requirement and made it into a group exercise in personal and social education.

A final example is the daily routine of calling the register. Undoubtedly the regular register-checking is very important, both for the care of the tutee and the legal requirement on the school. So enshrined is this in professional mythology that 'taking the register' is the jargon phrase in some schools synonymous with 'lead a tutorial session', as if the register check were the only activity. Even with the range of ICT registration in most secondary schools and the support of attendance officers, the mechanical 'checking' can force the developmental tutorial concept to one side. In many tutor groups the tutees are seated silently with no activity and no announcement of a topic or introduction to think about: then each name is ritually called and answered. In others, though, while the same message of the importance of the

## ELECTIONS TO THE SCHOOL COUNCIL

You will be voting for two students from your Tutor Group to be Student Representatives on the School Council. The Representatives – one girl and one boy – will speak on behalf of the whole tutor group, making suggestions about how to improve the school and solve problems.

Here are some qualities that the Class Representative might have. How do you rate these qualities?

| Are they: | VERY IMPORTANT | IMPORTANT | NOT IMPORTANT |
| --- | --- | --- | --- |
| a) Strong and physically fit | | | |
| b) Good with words | | | |
| c) Respected by the class | | | |
| d) Respected at listening to other people's opinions | | | |
| e) Good at explaining his/her opinion | | | |
| f) Good looking | | | |
| g) Smartly dressed | | | |
| h) Punctual | | | |

Supposing the school made a new rule that next term all girls would have to wear a school tie, as they do in some other schools.

Here are some things that a Student Representative might do. What does your group think of these ideas?

a) Tell everyone in the class what she/he thought.

b) Ask all the girls what they thought about the new rule, and report to the School Council.

c) Ask girls and boys what they thought about the new rule, and report to the School Council.

d) Not speak to anyone about the new rule.

e) Give his/her opinion to the Head of Textiles.

f) Give his/her opinion at the School Council, without asking what anyone else thought.

Figure 2   Worksheet for choosing a representative

accurate check by a designated time is conveyed, the tutees are welcomed first by a reminder about the purpose of that session: 'Today we are continuing our work on how to make complaints effectively.' A task or material to consider awaits them on the board, on the overhead projector or on a hand-out. After an introduction to this stage of the topic and the setting of a simple thought-provoking task, the tutor says: 'While you're working out which of those you think would offend least, I'll be checking the register and collecting notes from the two of you absent yesterday.' Thus the register administration is deftly knitted into the tutorial session.

Thus the art of the management of the tutor group is either to subordinate the administration to the tutorial task or, better still, use it as part of the heart of tutoring.

## Short tutorials

The problem of administrative routines dominating a tutorial session is especially so in the often daily short tutorial sessions. In most schools there is a short afternoon tutorial, often called 'registration'. Usually, this starts the afternoon – perhaps because a central government statutory order requires the register to be checked at the start of the afternoon. (This, however, does not have to be with the tutor, but can be part of the first course-department subject lesson, which is easier to administer with electronic equipment and procedures.) Some schools prefer a final 'tutorial' at the end of the afternoon, incorporating a check of who is there of course (as *every* session of every sort must do), but more importantly having the specific functions of:

- 'putting the day together', and reflecting on it
- looking ahead to homework, and preparing for it
- touching on tomorrow and the next days in the light of today's reflection

The points made in the last section on 'registration' especially apply in these short sessions: just 'calling the register' has virtually no pastoral curriculum content. What do the tutees *learn* from the thousandth calling out of their names? The task is necessary for the crucial tutorial activity of monitoring attendance, and some points can be made from it, e.g. a reprimand to a tutee without an absence note can be a prompt for a very brief general aphorism on keeping people in touch and on responsibility.

However, these short sessions need to be for more than entering the monitoring of attendance. The tutor cannot day after day hold the tutees in silence, with no activity but to listen to others' names being called out! Rather, the tutorial programme should be in the tutor's mind, and just as a good science teacher will use every moment to exercise the pupils' minds scientifically, so the ingenious tutor uses these moments. This means giving the tutor group a thinking, reading or writing activity to carry out while the names are being called.

Such activities require the bringing together of inventiveness, knowledge of the tutees, and deep, underpinning vision of the role of the tutor and pastoral care. The next section discusses tutorial activities in general. Even the shortest session can have a task that will contribute to the overall tutorial aim:

- 'Each of you think what was best about today.'
- 'Write down any word any member of the group used today that could have upset anyone.'
- 'Tomorrow is your parents' consultation evening meeting: what will you suggest your parent ask?'
- 'Write down what you remember most from this morning's assembly.'
- 'Last week, Armin was in a lot of trouble in many lessons. How has he managed this week?'

And so on! Even in the shortest session and even during a roll call thoughts can be formulated so that just before the pips go the tutor can transfer a roll call into a tutorial session – and the tutees learn a small but deeply important thought.

## Tutorial activities

Many of the units in tutorial programmes are planned to stimulate activity by the tutees. There is, of course, no virtue in activity for activity's sake: perhaps in search of peace we too often mistake mere doing for real learning. It is especially important in tutorial work that the tutee's *understanding* is engaged at as deep a level as possible. The tutor needs to select activities that will stimulate a consideration and reconsideration by the tutee of her attitudes and perceptions. For instance, many tutors would start Year 7 with the aim of developing an understanding of the new pupil's school and how a pupil can begin to make best use of it. The approach is not overtly explanatory but takes the tutee via an active reflection on previous visits to the school, comparisons of expectation, how it is turning out, and the working of how to help each other. Such a unit, therefore, must have a range of simple and easy-to-handle things for the tutees to do: questions, small investigations, and making plans. The activity of questioning others is designed to deepen the understanding of self. Quick advice and short-circuited ways round the almost inevitable difficulties of a new school should be complemented by the inner reflection that changes attitudes – and which makes this experience more than just getting settled into a school: it is, as so much group tutorial work, a paradigm for life.

One way to prompt reflection about behaviour is to set out in writing a situation and ask the tutees to write or describe his or her likely response. Then, two or more tutees discuss and evaluate each other's written reactions. For instance, a Year 8 group was asked:

See what you think is the most likely response you would make to the following situations. When you have finished, get a friend to check what you have written and see if you have been accurate and honest. You can do the same for her or him.

1. Everyone in the class is told off and given a detention for misbehaviour, but you know you were working perfectly well.
2. You are told off quite rightly for not completing your homework but you do not like the teacher anyway and you feel fed-up.
3. You are frantically finishing off a piece of work you have enjoyed when it is you who is asked to collect up everyone's books before the end of the lesson.

4. You have been getting into trouble for not having a pen with you, but this time it really is not your fault – you have a good excuse – but nobody is interested!

The emphasis given by the tutor has to be on the *honesty* of the tutee's speculation, not on the correctness of the response. The key activity is 'get a friend to check what you have written and see if you have been accurate and honest'. This is what needs most time and will both depend on the tutor-group atmosphere and trust and, very importantly, will contribute to it by increasing self- and mutual understanding.

Activities must not be merely text and worksheet-based. Indeed, relating to people is self-evidently a necessary way of developing *social* education. Sometimes tutees should be relating to each other in simple simulations: 'You are . . . and have to greet . . .' Whenever possible, though, there should be interaction with people outside the group: other students, staff of the school, and visitors. Greeting, briefing, interviewing and introducing are important learning experiences that embody aspects of the curriculum content of pastoral care.

As often as possible the activities should be real: boredom by a thousand simulations is all too easy. For instance, there will be members in hospital, families ready for celebrations, members of staff needing help, members of the community offering help. Phone-calls, letters, visits, and visitors need planning, carrying out and reflecting on.

Very few of the activities suggested in the units of any tutorial programme will be found difficult to handle in the tutor room; indeed most of them are within the normal repertoires of subject teachers. However, many tutors may not have experience of deploying the full range of the repertoire of teaching techniques or of moving from one technique to another so flexibly as is required for tutoring. The activities of the tutor group should have a contrasting range: reading, individual writing, small-group discussion, paired discussion, investigation. The inventiveness of the tutor's course-subject specialism can be utilized in devising these assignments. Tutors will normally find it best to exploit this variety so as to vary the *texture* of the tutorial sessions: it is easy to slip into a repetitive routine in which every session feels the same to your tutees – read, talk, write, for instance, in an invariable sequence.

The skilled tutor will deploy a varied repertoire of activities that develop the personal growth of the tutees.

## Paired and small-group work

Most, but not all, subject teachers use small-group work for discussion and planning. However, each subject tends to have its own convention and purpose for this. Teachers of Design and Technology, for instance, are used to groups of two or three, planning design solutions to specific briefs. Often such discussion work is very good in DT courses, perhaps because of the clarity of the end-product required: an agreed design or evaluation. Such teachers will bring especial skills to the tutorial but may find the purpose of some of the tutorial discussion tasks harder to handle as they may appear more intangible.

There is the fundamental question of why put the tutees into groups? What are we aiming at? What is intended? Are the tutees merely expected to work in groups or to do group-work? 'Working in groups' is a mere description of the placement of pupils. 'Group work' is the use of the group experience as a resource for the learning of its members. For a task to be carried out together is, of course, acceptable. On the other hand when students are deliberately expected to interact with one another, share a common aim, and jointly reflect on their achievement, something else is happening: the members of the group are learning something about and from the group itself. In these cases, the group, its members and their interaction are part of the learning material as well as the method.

The tutor planning an assignment will not let the tutees break into groups as a matter of habit, but will use the tutor room as a laboratory of pastoral care, the group as both scientist and material, finding ways of using the group to increase personal and inter-personal understanding.

The first question about small-group work is the composition of the groups. Most tutors let their tutees choose their own seats and thus most neighbours are self-chosen friendship groups. For some discussions this is helpful – the pupils already know each other well. On other occasions, though, this old familiarity acts as an unseen barrier to fresh thinking: the well-established friends have stereotypical views of each other, have cast each other into permanent roles, and cannot bring fresh responses to the focus of the work. They are sure to know each other so well there is no re-knowing possible; they have had so many personal and jokey conversations that they cannot bring a new language to analyse their behaviour.

It is wise, therefore, to establish early in tutorial work that there will be a variety of groupings, and explain why this is good. Sometimes they will be self-chosen and at other times the tutor will choose. Sometimes the tutor will choose at random and at other times deliberately pair those who do not usually work together. Pupils can become unwitting prisoners of their 'best friends' and the exploration of much tutorial activity needs to work outside as well as inside these established friendship patterns. Sometimes they will be mixed-sex groups and sometimes single-sex.

There is a temptation for self-chosen groups to have one or two well-known loquacious pupils and a very quiet one. It can be good for reticent pupils to be in with the verbally assured, but it can also inhibit them further. Putting two normally silent pupils together for an assignment virtually forces each of them to talk. Thus a variety of criteria should be used in composing groups for working – routine composition can be unwise.

Logically, the mode of grouping should reflect the purpose of the activity. On occasions, arbitrary random groups will work, for instance for devising a solution to a life-skills problem. On other occasions self-chosen groups work better. The key is to ensure that the group has a task, briefing, materials and a composition that encourage mutual scrutiny and understanding.

## Circle Time

One organizational technique of classroom management that is especially useful for the personal and social development of the pupils in a tutor period is what has come to be called 'Circle Time'. The idea developed by Jenny Mosley is to create for occasions of exploratory discussion and sharing a classroom pattern

and procedures that give 'emotional safety'. The unusual convention of sitting in a single circle, with 'ground rules established
for respectful listening' encourages a range of individual contributions and respectful listening, The following brief summary
can well be followed up in Jenny Mosley and Marilyn Tew's full-
length study: *Quality Circle Time in the Secondary School* (1999),
from which the quotations have been taken. How to listen and
how to learn from listening are the core of circle time, enabled by
the pupils being given a time and a format 'explicitly to socialise
with each other'.

Often introducing a new pattern of classroom arrangements and
procedures break the habitual classroom inter-personal ways of
going on and enable new behaviour relationships to develop. Of
course, not all problems are solved, but most can be. The classic
Circle Time convention is 'motivation by praise' and 'pupils learn
that the way to get noticed is by keeping the ground rules'.

Teachers and pupils need to agree:

- not to interrupt each other
- to signal if they wish to speak
- not to use put-downs (either verbal or non-verbal) towards
  each other
- if anyone does not wish to speak, he/she may say 'Pass'
- at the end of the round anyone who chose not to speak can
  be given a second opportunity
- not to name anyone in a negative way. Instead they must
  say 'Someone constantly takes my equipment' or 'Some
  people push into the queue'. Similarly, the circle rules
  enable pupils to respect the privacy of their families. As in
  all situations when personal matters are being discussed,
  pupils must be reminded that if they want to tell you
  anything of a serious nature, they should use private, one-
  to-one time. Make sure that you warn pupils that if they
  ever choose to tell you anything through the listening
  systems that causes you concern, you may have to take it
  further

(*op. cit.*, pp. 48–49)

There is a fixed pattern of seating in a circle and fixed procedures: a three-phase pattern of 'introductory, including warm-up
games and rounds; middle-phase – open forum; close phase, which
can include celebrations of success and closing forms or rituals'.

We have observed that a routine use of the Circle Time
conventions, say once a fortnight in one of the longer tutorial
sessions, brings the pupils into a different vision of their concerns
and a fresh perspective on sharing their feelings. Encouragingly
*Guideline Notes* from the DfEE in 1999 declared:

> The Whole School Quality Circle Time Model . . . can help
> improve and maintain high standards of behaviour and dis-
> cipline.
>
> (DfEE, 1999, p. 7)

Pupil grouping and discussion routines are a consideration for all
teaching opportunities. The tutor sessions, with their breadth and
depth of explorations and ambitions require the imaginative and
practical use of the full range of pupil-grouping and discussion
routine plans.

## Assignments

If we are not careful and ingenious, the tutee can pass through a
battery of assignments but not always grasp the purpose. The difficult
art in planning, explaining and managing an assignment is to ensure
the tutee derives the deeper gain from the tasks in the assignment.

In setting discussion assignments, tutors will need to use the
precision of a science or humanities teacher in making clear what
the *point* is and to what *product* the discussion is to lead. In the
apparently intangible world of personal and social development, it
is too tempting to let every conversation be about very similar
things and for routine remarks to be rehearsed. Hence the wording
of the discussion assignments has to be very carefully sharpened.
Specific targets are normally better than the broad exhortation:
'Discuss!' For instance, a Year 9 tutorial topic was on the broad
aspect of how one can 'learn from experience'. After the tutor's
introductory exposition, the group discussion assignment was in a
briefing sheet for each discussion group:

**What helps you look forward to new experiences?**

In your groups discuss how important you think the following points are:

1. It is important to congratulate yourself when you have done something new. Or something that you are proud of.
2. Encouragement from others is more likely to help you see your way forward.
3. Friends around you who are willing to join in and share new activities with you often act as a support.
4. If you trust the people you are with then you are more likely to experiment and still feel safe.

Tutors would be well advised to highlight the focus of the task 'Discuss how important you think the following points are', and not use the text as a mere springboard for a general discussion on new experiences.

Guidance can be given from time to time on discussion methods. For instance, one of the hardest intellectual tasks for the secondary student is to move away from a narrative-dominated way of speaking to a more abstract analytic mode in which the anecdote is an illustration, not an end in itself. Children are great, if sometimes interminable, storytellers. Do not let the tutorial work sink under a string of episodes!

# 4 From exhortation to enabling

## Introduction

Childhood is a journey through admonition, exhortation and advice. School intensifies these elements, and the tutor can easily become chief exhorter – not only with her own demands but also as a mouthpiece for the massed complaints of numerous subject teachers! Yet a barrage of exhortation is unlikely to change the tutee, except at the margins and for a few, and the tutor session risks becoming little more than a tirade of such exhortation.

Many subject teachers often look to those with pastoral responsibilities to keep their pupils under control. They nobble you at coffee time, or send notes declaring: 'That Janice of yours is wasting her time in my lessons – and making my teaching difficult. Do something about it!' Often they want immediate results without any inner development or, equally perversely, expect wholesale changes in character or personality!

This is a major example of how the tutor can be overburdened by the immediate 'business' of the job and tempted to abandon the educational core of the tutorial role.

Much of the art of tutoring is foreseeing likely problems and finding active and thought-provoking ways to prepare for them. The exhortation or warning is necessary ('when you find . . .' or 'don't whatever you do . . .'), but not sufficient. Tutors need to help tutees analyse situations and devise strategies for themselves.

Of course, this does not just apply to difficulties and things that go wrong. The tutorial programme that portrays life as a series of trials, with 'problems' of drink, drugs, sex, indiscipline, and anxiety as the landmarks of growing up, is both inaccurate and unhelpful – and all too common!

Conversely, the work of a tutor group should look forward to and relish the quiet pleasures and excitements of life. For morality is not a torture of admonitions, but a growth through the satisfaction of enlightened choice; relationships are not a catalogue of difficulties, but a revelation of fulfilment and reciprocity.

## Learning about learning

One of the most important aspects of the tutor's role is helping pupils to see how to make good use of teachers, teaching assistants, support staff, resources and the organization of the school. In many ways, the school is a microcosm of society's large bureaucracies of, for example, the health service, local councils, the police, banks and other major corporations. Teaching pupils to understand and use the school organization also gives them the tools to use these other bureaucracies.

Such tutoring is best done by a combination of group sessions in the tutorial programme and of individual advice and counselling on coping with staff, on handling routines and on making choices. A central part of this is assisting pupils to reflect on their lessons, the teachers' aims, the methods used, and each pupil's learning approach and success. However, a tutorial session must focus on this in a way that is more than a jocular repetition of conventional pupil jibes. For example, pupils and teachers lack a shared technical language for talking about pedagogy. The pupils' vernacular ('boring' or 'just keep writing') is both insufficiently comprehensive or precise. Ironically, teachers' jargon has the same failings; few of us engage in classroom analysis of teaching and much of our vocabulary is vague: for example, the much-used phrase 'discussion work'.

The form tutor is really the best-placed adult in the school to help the pupils make connections between different aspects of the curriculum. Further, although all subject-course teachers should include aspects of approaches to learning in their teaching, the form tutor has the school-wide responsibility for her or his tutees that gives a special responsibility for helping each pupil develop their learning styles and study strategies.

Professor Jean Rudduck, director of research at Homerton College at the University of Cambridge, experimented with preparing pupils for a pedagogical change to enquiry-based history learning by holding a special conference for the pupils. She criticized her own arrangements for not providing a way to analyse and discuss teaching and learning. Subsequently, she observed:

> Pupils noticed – but did not discuss with their teacher – occasional shortcomings in the new teaching style: 'When we first started we didn't do any writing – no writing at all. He just talked to us. It was rather boring.' The pupils were not able to go further. What they lacked was a shared language for talking about the new pedagogy – the reflexive language of critique which seems to come from the analysis of oneself and one's peers at work.
>
> (Rudduck, 1983, p. 40)

Pupils need, if they are to be successful *pupils*, 'the readiness and the words to talk publicly about learning' (*op. cit.*, p. 41). Part of the tutorial programme is to provide this possibility.

The tutor group is also the laboratory for understanding about learning. Pupils bring expectations of what 'lessons' are going to be like, indeed *should* be like. For example, pupils coming to secondary school for the first time have strong ideas about how 'difficult' work will be – and are often disappointed. A key tutorial task, therefore, is to help pupils understand their expectations and match them against the teachers' plans.

Ideally, the tutor should work with her subject colleagues in preparing for change. Jean Rudduck has highlighted the conservatism of pupil groups:

> Pupils, however, are not without power, and their power, which is rooted in long experience of teachers and teaching, can be used to protect themselves against change. If the norms of classroom behaviour are suddenly changed and a new mode of learning introduced, then it is not surprising if pupils seek to reinstate the familiar, the comfortably predictable, and through the power of group pressure lure the teacher back into recognisable routines. Pupils can represent, albeit unwittingly, a conservative force in the classroom.
>
> (Rudduck, 1983, p. 32)

The tutor can harness this 'long experience of teachers and teaching' to help the tutees to become more conscious of it, unpick it, and consider the component parts – and, above all, help them to control their contribution to the 'group pressure'.

The most telling, and increasingly familiar, justification for focusing on learning about learning comes from a pupil: 'It's not that I haven't learnt much. It's just that I don't really understand what I'm doing' (Rudduck, Wallace and Harris, 1995). One of the most coherent definitions of learning about learning, or meta-learning, is:

> Learning is the process of creating knowledge by making sense of your experience. Meta-learning is the process of making sense of your experience of learning.
>
> (Watkins *et al.*, 1998)

Each of us makes sense of our experience of learning in different ways, and each of us has a 'preferred learning style'. When a pupil's own learning style is not similar to the standard classroom approach, he or she can fall behind. Tutors need to understand their own preferred learning style, before moving on to helping their tutees reach a similar understanding about how each learns best and most enjoyably. In this way, teachers can cater for different styles in the way they teach and the activities they offer to pupils. Similarly, tutors can adapt, say, their mentoring approach to suit the tutee's own style of learning.

The reasons for this variety in how we learn are now well known – for example, the 'rational' left-brain and 'creative' right-brain activity; Howard Gardner's multiple intelligences, each of which we make use of to varying degrees; and emotional intelligence as defined by Daniel Goleman.

However, Gardner himself issues a warning about misinterpreting or misappropriating such scientific theories. He has talked of 'the confusion of intelligences with learning styles and the confounding of human intelligence with a societal domain (e.g. musical intelligence being equated with mastery of a certain musical genre or role)' (Gardner, 2003). He concludes:

> 'Multiple intelligences' should not in and of itself be an educational goal. Educational goals need to reflect one's own

values, and these can never come simply or directly from a scientific theory. Once one reflects on one's educational values and states one's educational goals, however, then the putative existence of our multiple intelligences can prove very helpful. And, in particular, if one's educational goals encompass disciplinary understanding, then it is possible to mobilise our several intelligences to help achieve that lofty goal.

(Gardner, 2003)

This suggests that a tutor's most effective approach might be to become familiar with these various theories, and to draw on them as the learning style of a tutee develops and becomes explicit.

An effective learner understands the processes involved in learning and can apply that across a range of learning contexts. The National Association for Pastoral Care in Education (NAPCE) has provided one suitable framework within which this might be carried out. For example, it defines the role of the tutor here as:

to provide the necessary structures for pupils to progress through the learning cycle: setting up the initial tasks, handling the review, extracting the learning, and encouraging application. In all phases this requires the teacher to display skilled steering of the event, and to play a key role in making meaning and making connections. Teachers can make their specialist input through these processes. Facilitating learning through this cycle is, at its best, a highly structured (but still open-ended) process.

(Watkins *et al.*, 1998)

The learning cycle referred to comprises:

| *task* | *tutor's role* |
| --- | --- |
| **Doing** | encourage and support tutee to engage in activities, tasks and processes |
| **Reviewing** | facilitate reflection, discussion and feedback; and support emergence of new understandings and insights, and tutee's evaluation of strategies |

**Learning**   help tutee to make the learning explicit, draw out insights and understandings from the review stage; compare current strategies and revise and develop them for the next stage

**Applying**   help tutee to plan future action in light of new understanding by promoting transfer of learning, planning for specific situations, and setting goals

The cycle can be started at any one of the four stages.

The review element of this cycle needs to take account of each tutee's preferred learning style. NAPCE breaks this down into four aspects which are, briefly:

**concrete experience**
involving oneself in new experiences

**reflective observation**
wanting to understand the meaning of ideas and situations

**abstract conceptualisation**
using logic, ideas and concepts

**active experimentation**
trying out ideas, theories and techniques in practice

These create useful connections with Howard Gardner's set of multiple intelligences:

**Verbal/Linguistic**
ability with spoken and written words and language

**Musical**
sensitivity to sounds, tones, pitch, melody, rhythms and beats

**Logical/Mathematical**
reasoning (inductive and deductive), scientific and logical thinking, abstract concepts, hypothesising, testing, drawing conclusions, calculating, and recognising patterns

**Visual/Spatial**
ability to visualise, create internal mental images, manipulate images and objects in space, identify visual and spatial patterns and relationships

**Bodily/Kinaesthetic**

physical movement and body awareness, and expressed through dance, sport, body language and exercise

**Inter-personal**

interpersonal interaction, relationships and communication, learn in groups, work on collaborative projects, and learn by talking and interacting with others

**Intra-personal**

reflection, metacognition (thinking about thinking), self-awareness, a focus on feelings and a sense of spirituality, like to work alone, reflect, process information emotionally and cognitively and able to concentrate well

It is important for such a policy as learning about learning to be integral to a school as a whole, and for everyone to be involved in the learning conversation. In many respects, learning about learning embodies core elements of the tutor/tutee relationship, and one in particular: collaboration. It is learning about, sharing and building on how each other works. It is remembering that 'none of us is as smart as all of us' (Bennis and Biederman, 1997).

# Homework

Homework is an obvious example of the tutor's dilemma of having to deal with the immediate business of school life at the same time as sustaining the educational core of tutoring.

The tutor must, of course, support colleagues and help pupils to meet their educational targets. However, the tutor's central task is not merely to ensure this or that piece of homework is set or completed on time. Rather, it is the educational task of enabling each pupil to understand her- or himself and develop the skills to make decisions and take control of time and self. This will not be helped by retrospective chiding prompted by displeased subject teachers. The tutor needs to look ahead and help the tutee to think and internalize an understanding of how to handle the challenge of the difficult.

For example, the tutor of year 7 group led a session early in the new term in which he asked each pupil to review the last few days:

- How much time had each pupil given to the assignments?
- Which pupils had not completed a piece of work?
- What had caused difficulties?

The tutor wrote on the board a list of the reasons given and the group discussed the justification for each reason, getting the tutor to erase each rejected reason. The tutor also prepared a multi-choice worksheet (see below) and the tutees, working in small groups, debated the pros and cons of each answer. They were, in effect, considering and devising planning behaviour. You will see that while there are some readily discardable answers, many need pondering.

---

### Homework

Your teacher has not set any homework. Do you:
(a) keep quiet, hoping he has forgotten?
(b) ask for some?
(c) write 'none set'?
(d) do your own for half an hour?

You can't copy down the work in time. Do you:
(a) try to remember it?
(b) tell your tutor?
(c) not do the homework?
(d) ask the teacher to write it up earlier next time?

When do you do it?
(a) whenever you feel like it
(b) while watching TV
(c) the same time each night
(d) when you are told to

Where do you do it?
(a) in your room alone
(b) in the library
(c) at a friend's home
(d) in the same room as the TV

> Who helps?
> (a) nobody, you just hand in what you can do
> (b) you get help before you start
> (c) you show it to someone to check after you finish
> (d) you copy the bits you couldn't do from a friend

Time does not allow such a full session of analysis every week. But there are periods, such as early in year 8 – that time of a possible lull in enthusiasm – when the tutor would want to ask tutees in a structured way to reconsider their approaches to homework (see below).

Over the run of a term, of course, the tutor would need to encourage further the kind of thinking and self-scrutiny explored in such a session – for example, by using a few moments at the end of the day to establish the group's assignments; having tutees look at each other's work at the start of the day; and arranging for various members of the group to be in charge of certain reminders.

The art, though, is to avoid merely harrying and to enable the tutees to think and plan.

## Information and study skills

The tutor's work enabling the tutee to learn more effectively will often, quite properly, engage with the more immediate realities of a particular problem of procedure, of an individual assignment, of an individual teacher, or a detailed skill. The previous account of developing approaches to homework, however, shows that the tutor can move from the particular to the general, and back again. Without being able to stand back, contemplate, analyse and generalize before re-engaging, the tutor risks providing pupils with only a reactive and fragmented series of raids on the coasts of learning, and leaving the heartlands unpenetrated and the landscape unmapped.

The real tutorial task is deeper and wider than that – and much more difficult. The tutor must enable pupils to rise above the immediate needs of one assignment after another and to understand, and take control of, their own learning process – in short, learn how to study.

Ideally, the individual subject teacher will be giving clear instruction and practice on the skills required by pupils for each task at the right time and in the relevant context. Usually, though, such tuition is given solely in the context of a particular task rather than helping pupils to find a way to generalize. Rare is the pupil who will develop her own understanding of what is required and create, almost spontaneously, an analysis and a synthesis. These will be the successful pupils – the more so as they reach higher levels.

For most pupils, though, this will not happen unless the school includes in the curriculum a specific understanding of information skills – that is, as an intended learning outcome. The good teacher of history is one who thinks about issues, assesses evidence, searches out arguments, and arranges ideas and information in history. Similarly, the good teacher of science is teaching not only the answers of science, but more importantly, the method of handling scientific enquiries, the preliminary thinking towards a hypothesis, the literature search for current knowledge, the devising of an enquiry, and the weighing of evidence.

The term 'information skills' was first widely used to cover the intellectual tasks at the heart of most assignments – from simple homework pieces to lengthy GCSE or A level research studies – that involve posing a question, seeking evidence, and reporting on it (see Marland, *Information Skills in the Secondary Curriculum*, 1981). These skills have a remarkable stability across the subjects, and might more readily be thought of as a key curriculum skill.

Indeed, since the Education Act 2002, there is a real sense in which a whole range of adult activities from, say, writing this book to preparing an oral presentation to a staff committee, parallels the stream of tasks set throughout the secondary school. Each can be seen as having in it the same sequence of question steps, even though some assignments speed simply through some steps and enlarge the importance of others.

The major impetus for the development of information skills came from a 1981 British Library/Schools Council working party (see Marland, 1981). This set out a series of nine steps or questions for a school's information skills curriculum. Despite considerable debate both about the concept and the content of such skills (see Rogers, *Teaching Information Skills*, 1994), these nine steps have remained at the heart of common thinking about learning how to study.

## Nine Questions for Handling Information

| | |
|---|---|
| 1 **What do I need to do?** | Formulate and analyse need |
| 2 **Where could I go?** | Identify and appraise likely information resources |
| 3 **How do I get the information?** | Locate individual resources |
| 4 **Which resources should I use?** | Examine, select, and reject individual resources |
| 5 **How shall I use the resources?** | Interrogate resources |
| 6 **What should I make a record of?** | Record and store information |
| 7 **Have I got the information I need?** | Interpret, analyse, synthesize and evaluate information |
| 8 **How should I present it?** | Shape, present and communicate information |
| 9 **What have I achieved?** | Evaluate the assignment |

Ideally, there should be a whole-school policy on teaching information skills, with specific tuition and practice in most of the timetabled subjects. This is an example of one of the key elements for developing the National Curriculum and its foundation subjects, whereby 'other subjects and cross-curricular themes can and should figure in schemes of work covering the whole curriculum' (DES, 1989, para 4.3). It has become an essential part of evaluating the quality and range of a school's curriculum in the Ofsted inspection process, which requires evidence of 'whole curriculum planning for National Curriculum subjects, non-National Curriculum subjects and cross-curricular themes' (Ofsted, 1993).

Such a policy has to be firmly rooted in the school development plan (Marland, 1981), but flexibly implemented to allow for the different 'styles' of individual subject teachers (Lincoln, 1987). Schools need to take account of the factors involved in achieving complex change. Any whole-school approach to information skills needs active and enthusiastic advocates, and should involve as many of the staff as possible through collaborative working and highlighting the benefits to each subject area (Howard, 1991). The critical factor will be the impact on the pupils of learning how to study effectively and their subsequent performance in other teachers' lessons.

The tutor, of course, plays the pivotal role in any whole-school approach. She must enable pupils to develop a central understanding of handling information and to focus on the range of skills required. At the same time, she must have a curriculum overview and bring to that the detailed knowledge of each of her tutees and their modes of working.

In consequence, the tutor is best placed to consolidate and make sense of the disparate learning experiences of the timetable. She can help a pupil to stand back, observe the techniques demanded by assignments in each subject, see what they have in common and how they differ, and make a coherent inner model of the information-handling process.

The tutor can start by gathering from pupils a selection of assignments from, say, science, history, technology and English:

- what is at the heart of each assignment?
- what have they got in common?
- how does one set about them?
- which is the most difficult stage in each?

For example, sometimes the most difficult part of an assignment is finding the sources of facts and ideas; at other times it is understanding the source material once it has been found, or knowing what to reject, or deciding in what order to re-arrange the facts and ideas.

In effect, the tutor invites the pupil to stand back from the subject, put aside the content, be free of the tension of completing the work, and instead to reflect on the process. In this way, the pupil can come to an understanding of the needs of assignments in general and of her own skills, and thus to take a grasp on learning.

Without needing specific subject knowledge or expertise, the tutor can concentrate on one of more of the Nine Questions (see page 64), and is uniquely placed within the school to compare and contrast these questions in the context of the different subjects.

For example, the tutor might spend a session on 'identifying and appraising likely sources of information' with such prompting questions as:

- where could I go?
- what sources are available when you are trying to find something out?
- when is it sensible to ask someone?
- who is it sensible to ask?
- when is quoting 'research' or 'scholarly' and when 'lazy' or even 'plagiarism'?
- what are the advantages of newspapers, journals and encyclopaedias?

Another session might be on 'what shall I make a record of?', asking:

- what forms of note-taking are there?
- when is photocopying better than note-taking?
- what are the advantages of lined paper against plain, card against paper, ring-binders against folders?
- what ways can be used to make the points noted easier to re-organize later?

Pupils can compare each other's recording techniques and describe what seem to be the good and bad points. There is no 'right' method, but pupils can be made more aware of the range of techniques and their advantages and disadvantages. For example:

- what ways are there for using the layout of the page to reveal the structure of the arguments being noted?
- what use can be made of upper- and lower-case letters, indentations and underlinings?

In all of this, the tutor will not be speaking as a subject specialist, and paradoxically will have the advantage of not knowing the subject content. She will be able to approach the range of assignments with something of the same perspectives as the pupil, and will sharpen comparisons between the stages of different assignments.

Wider study skills include:

- organizing time
- planning appropriate questions to ask when unsure or baffled
- recording ideas and facts that need to be to hand
- learning to remember what needs to be remembered
- reacting appropriately to assessment and real assignment requirements

In some schools, there may be specific short courses that are complementary to the work done by subject teachers. But the tutor will always have the integrative task of helping the pupil to find a coherent approach to 'learning to learn'.

## Facing and making use of criticism

Giving and receiving criticism can lead to much unhappiness and many rows. Too often we meet a pupil's inappropriate reaction to criticism only by reprimands or by would-be calming remarks. But how can pupils learn to accept, resolve and – most important of all – make best use of criticism?

A key situation here is how a pupil should respond if he considers a teacher has criticized him unfairly. The tutor can help pupils to accept that in all parts of their life – in school and outside, now and in the future – there is always the risk of being wrongly accused of something. Some everyday examples include the ticket collector calling back a season ticketholder for scrutiny, the police officer insisting on a breathalyser test, the shopkeeper querying the money offered by a customer. Within the family, both children and adults are sometimes thought to have offended when there has merely been a misunderstanding.

Someone has to negotiate these delicate moments, and the tutor group is one of the laboratories in which these negotiations can be experimented with and solutions discovered.

The wise tutor will prepare for such moments rather than focus discussion only on a retrospective examination of particular events. For example, text, video or anecdote can be used to help a group of pupils to imagine a particular moment. The pupils can then suggest a variety of responses and consider the benefits and problems of each. The tutor might sometimes propose a list of reactions on the board, on the overhead projector or in a hand-out; at other times, a list can be built up from the group's ideas.

Most pupils will approach such distanced episodes with a fair degree of objectivity. Dramatizing fiction, biography or video presentation allows the kind of objective identification described so well by Bertolt Brecht in his theory of the theatre. The actor does not 'become' the character, but 'demonstrates' it for the audience, who are not to 'identify' with the characters, but to 'consider' them.

The tutor's role in bringing narrative (through fiction or the moving image) into the tutorial period is like the role of the actors speaking the prologue in Brecht's play *The Exception and the Rule*, who exhort the audience:

> Observe the conduct of these people closely:
> Find it estranging even if not very strange,
> Hard to explain even if it is the custom
> Hard to explain even if it is the rule
> Observe the smallest action, seeming simple,
> With mistrust
> Enquire if a thing be necessary
> Especially if it is common
> We particularly ask you –
> When a thing continually occurs –
> Not on that account to find it natural.
>
> (Brecht, 1966)

However, the real and the immediate are also required. The wise tutor will use the inevitable episodes of school and of personal and family life to revisit the generalities with the sharply particular. A pupil might say: 'Wayne got into real trouble yesterday. But it wasn't fair because . . .' The tutor can have the tutorial group suggest advice for Wayne from their own feelings for his plight and from their earlier work on the 'distanced' event.

In a group that is working well, pupils can share how they feel when rebuked, discuss responses and compare them with their internal feelings: 'I just smiled at him, but inside I can tell you I was real hurt, shocked. He shouldn't have said it, but I wasn't going to let him know what he'd done to me inside!'

By talking through the reactions of characters in fiction or on video, pupils can relate their feelings to those of characters who, although fictional, prompt a fresh response. The criticized situations of pupils in school can be illuminated through observing others in fiction.

## 'It's not fair, Miss!'

Pupils will bring a miscellany of complaints about things 'not being fair' – some trivial, some plain wrong. But some accounts will be of real injustice. A reactive tutor makes sympathetic noises, brushes the matter aside, or just occasionally and with some embarrassment, takes up a major problem. A proactive tutor prepares for such occasions and uses them as they happen to enable a pupil to avoid such situations or to cope when they do occur.

Coping with a grievance is hard for all of us some of the time. But those who cannot handle a grievance well face a bitter paradox: the less well you can resolve a problem, the worse the grievance becomes. The repertoire of ineffective reactions to a grievance goes from reticent festering to loud-mouthed moaning. Young people can be particularly inept at expressing a complaint in an acceptable or positive way.

In one exercise of enabling, the tutor can address the general question of complaints:

- what makes someone cross with a person in authority?
- how can that complaint best be expressed?
- as the person being complained about, how would you feel if the aggrieved person described things in this way or that way?

Many pupils, who feel impotent fury if a teacher has in their view been 'unfair', let the matter fester because they do not know how to do otherwise. Through discussion, the tutor can help the pupil to imagine the other person's state of mind, and consider objectively how that person would hear and see possible reactions. For example, what are the different effects on a person of sentences starting:

- 'That's not fair!'
- 'I didn't do what you said I did yesterday.'
- 'Excuse me, Miss, could you please reconsider what you said yesterday?'
- 'I am sorry about yesterday, Sir, and I wonder if you have time for me to explain how I think it happened?'

One tutor asked his pupils to think of a really complicated situation over which they felt they had been unfairly treated. They then discussed what sort of letter they could send to the allegedly unfair teacher:

- what would be the best opening?
- what is the point of the conventional courtesies and the standard greeting ('Dear Mr Smith') when you are cross?
- for how much should you apologize – if at all?
- what are you asking should be done about the incident?

The tutor is helping the pupils to find a way ahead after difficulties, and to move the role from merely showing sympathy to providing support for the future.

The way in which pupils respond to the peer-group jibes of the playground or to the classroom and corridor complaints of teachers – to take just two examples from the range of behaviour for which tutors are responsible – will illustrate how well teachers in general and tutors in particular have prepared them for such challenges.

Our argument, therefore, is that how pupils respond to criticism is a product of how the school – and within that the pastoral team – has responded to and looked after its new pupils. The tutor enables the pupil to make a constructive response.

## The study of behaviour

The child coming into secondary school with behaviour problems almost always has a long history of difficulties with others going back to her or his earliest years. Extensive research demonstrates that many aspects of these difficulties derive from the beginning of childhood. The 'security of attachment' created by the child's mother – although the prime care-giver will not always be the child's biological mother – gives the young baby a sense of self-esteem, plants the ability to recognize effectively the other's concerns and motives, and teaches security and self-assessment. The greater the security of attachment that babies have, the more they develop a trust of others, interpret others' motives positively, and react to situations with understanding and confidence:

> Maternal sensitivity and responsiveness to an infant's signals during feeding, play, and distress during the course of the first three months were found to be predictive of the quality of the attachment at the end of the child's first year of life: mothers who showed insensitivity to their baby's signals in a variety of caretaking and play situations were more likely to have children who were later characterised as being insecurely attached, having a behaviour pattern which showed an insecure attachment pattern.
>
> (Belsky and Isabella, 1988)

As in the case of 'Reading Recovery', in which techniques are later taught that were not picked up by the child when young, so behavioural understanding and techniques can be taught to such a child. The loss of that early security of attachment training is serious, but major steps forward can be taken if the missing aspects are recognized and specifically taught. While specialist psychologists are required for the most serious difficulties, the ordinary classroom intervention by the teacher can give massive help to many children – and this is especially true of the tutor's integrative role.

However, teachers often find themselves telling pupils how their behaviour was wrong, without giving precepts about the future:

- to what extent does this flow of criticism enable a pupil to take control of her behaviour?
- how can the tutor use a tutorial programme to teach more about behaviour – its causes and effects, and how to adapt it?

Some people fear that considering behaviour would reduce humanity to performing roles in the procedures of outward etiquette. Most of us remember the repeated adult commands to 'speak nicely', 'don't do that', or 'say "please"'. Many teachers would equate any tutorial concentration on behaviour as just more of that.

Interestingly, there is clear evidence of a relationship between maladjustment and modes of expressing emotion. One of the unfairnesses of schooling is that some pupils come into school with an 'off-putting' style, mostly through an inappropriate vocal tone or facial expression. Sometimes, of course, it is appropriate to show displeasing emotions and to anticipate the reactions such emotions trigger. Even then, most of us would counsel some limitation on outward expression in the interest of working towards a positive resolution of the dispute. But the tutorial questions are:

- does the pupil realize what he is expressing?
- does he realize what effect that expression is having on others?
- is the pupil sufficiently self-conscious and self-controlling?

Many psychologists in the 1970s considered the child to be 'an intuitive psychologist' (Taylor and Harris, 1984, p. 141). They scrutinized those aspects of personality that affect so much and which we usually talk about only loosely – 'the child's knowledge of memory processes and rules for self-control'. Not surprisingly, it was shown that:

> Younger children know a good deal about the links between situations and the emotional reactions that they elicit. However, in contrast to children of ten years or more, they are less aware of the inner mental component to emotion, and of the possible conflict that can arise when one emotion is felt internally but another is displayed externally.
>
> (Taylor and Harris, 1984)

One element of the tutorial programme should make explicit the continuation of this growth:

- 'How do people often look if . . . ?'
- 'What do other people think if someone comes into a room with *this* expression?'

- 'Which of these facial expressions [selected from a range of photographs] would you display if a teacher accused you of rudeness when you hadn't said anything?'

Research has shown that the pupils who are less liked by their peers largely have a poor judgement of other people's facial expressions, and misjudge their feelings. It is interesting that the normal increase of understanding and the use of 'control strategies' as children get older was not the case for maladjusted boys in one research study. One possible intervention strategy, set out below, offers 'prompts' to help the less socially adjusted. Could not the tutorial programme help all pupils to develop their understanding and control?

> The results indicate that normal and maladjusted boys differ in the strategies they propose for reacting to provocation but not the emotion that they expect to feel. It is tempting to conclude that maladjusted boys lack knowledge of control strategies. However, it could also be argued that while they know of such strategies, they find them difficult to apply in practice or choose to adopt counter-aggression instead. Indeed, it is noteworthy that slightly more than half of the maladjusted boys who failed to offer a control strategy spontaneously did offer one in reply to the experimenter's prompt.
>
> (Taylor and Harris, 1984, p. 144)

There is also a fair body of research evidence to support the 'common-sense' view that the effects of young people's own behaviour influences other people's responses to them, and that in turn affects the future behaviour of the young people themselves. 'Oppositional children elicit different types of behaviour than do passive compliant children . . . Aggressive boys tend to elicit negative behaviour from their peers' (Rutter, 1989, p. 41). The tutor can enable pupils to understand and influence this by their behaviour.

# Bullying

Bullying, in all its various forms including racial and sexual harassment, is prevalent in schools as in other institutions in society. As
with child abuse in the home, studies continue to show a higher
rate of bullying in schools than most of us had assumed.

Every teacher will intervene when she sees evidence of bullying,
stop the trouble and reprimand the pupils who appear to be the
aggressors. Tutors who hear of one of their pupils being bullied
will also be sympathetic and supportive to the victim.

Such responses are necessary but not sufficient: they attempt to
cope with the immediate needs but are not 'educational' in that
they offer little opportunity for bully or victim to learn for the
future.

The tutor, of course, should not work in isolation over bullying,
and the contribution of the tutor group should be one component
in a whole-school policy which would include:

- the school ethos and atmosphere
- inter-staff and staff–pupil relationships
- supervisory systems, with special emphasis on the dangerous
  times, (e.g. dinner break and after school) and places (e.g.
  toilets and back corridors)
- a behaviour code devised by pupils, staff and parents
- a proper consideration of language, including how it carries
  association and offence
- an anti-racist policy
- a programme for building individual and school esteem

Whether or not there is such a whole-school policy, the tutor
can make a major contribution to enabling both potential bully and
potential victim to alter their behaviour. Overall, two forces affect
the level and intensity of bullying: the social and architectural
environment working inwards; and the inner psychology of victim
and bully working outwards.

While bullying is clearly 'pathological' behaviour, its frequency
makes it difficult to call it firmly 'deviant' behaviour. The danger is
that considerations of the undoubted fact that 'bullying obviously
meets a need' could appear to legitimize it. The tutor's aim is to

speculate what needs are being serviced by unpleasant behaviour and ask how those needs can be 'serviced' by non-pathological means.

In working from exhortation against bullying to enabling pupils to reduce or remove it, tutors need to focus on the following elements:

## How the group can help

In probably the best essay on the school and bullying, Graham Herbert describes 'a whole-curriculum approach to bullying', and concludes with the emphasis on mobilizing the peer group:

> Perhaps the most important factor in combating bullying is the social pressure brought to bear by the peer group rather than the condemnation of individual bullies by someone in authority.
>
> (Herbert, 1989, p. 82)

This is a clear example of working away from mere exhortation. One useful exercise is for a tutor group to imagine that a new pupil joins the group and finds older pupils from other groups being beastly to him. 'How', asks the tutor, 'would you respond to seeing this happen?'

The tutor can use the group's coherence and initial support that he has nurtured to enable the group to develop its dislike of and refusal to accept bullying.

## Changing vocabulary

Children have used the word since they first spoke, and 'You bully!' is a frequent phrase. But it is rare for them to have analysed bullying disinterestedly, and separately from a personal incident (as fits well in, for example, science, history or English literature), and to define and analyse cause and effect, and consider strategies of response.

Ideally, questions of violence and power that crop up in time-tabled subjects, such as social studies, literature, media studies and drama, should be related by those subject teachers to individuals. However, the tutor's task is to bring all aspects together and help pupils to see what is happening behind the show of violence.

In addition, the offensiveness of offensive language should be analysed by linguistic experts in English or languages lessons. Rather than adults baldly and repetitively admonishing children not to use 'bad language', children should be helped to understand why it is 'bad'. For example, why, according to one dictionary of slang, are there 68 words to use for a woman judged to be promiscuous and just 9 for a man? Why is 'Paki' offensive when 'Pakistani' is appropriately descriptive?

The tutor's task is to focus objectively on the language of the group and enable them to face up to the casual use of offensive language and its effects. The tutor can help the group towards a policy of its own, particularly for racist and sexist abuse. Pupils are empowered by knowledge and by realizing they can adjust their vocabulary. The admonition 'control yourself' is good sense, but is empty unless the tutor has empowered the pupil with the means to do it.

### Assertiveness and life skills

It is dangerously tempting sometimes to blame the victim: 'Why did he act like that?' In avoiding this trap, the tutor should not ignore the possibility of enabling pupils to develop fresh skills of communication to fend off the potential difficulty. These skills include controlling facial expression, body language, tone of voice and style of language. In essence, this is 'assertiveness training' – not making people more aggressive but the opposite: enabling someone to make their point, reject the unpleasant and avoid being hurt without being aggressive. The tutor, both with the tutor group as a whole and in individual counselling, can help pupils consider how their manner can keep their end up.

### Understanding and practising skills

The tutor can help pupils practise ways of speaking. Ask the group to think how they would say, for example, 'That's not true' when they are (a) angry, (b) bored, (c) confident. After each pupil says the words, the rest of the group put their hands up to show which tone they thought was *intended*.

- Did the speaker give the wrong impression – if so, how?
- How could it be changed?

Experience from extensive observation and many drama lessons reveals that secondary pupils appear to show less control over their voices than over their facial expressions. They can, for example, answer a straightforward question with a tone of voice that inadvertently suggests 'what a stupid question!' But they can be helped to listen to each other and to themselves, and to shape their voice to their intention. This is, of course, a part of most aspects of handling their lives, but is also crucial in having the greatest chance of avoiding being bullied.

## Handling the bully

If a potential or actual bully is in your tutor group, it is unlikely that you will want to handle all the implications yourself; you will no doubt wish to consult your team leader. In the context of this chapter on exhortation to enabling, the tutor's task is to help the pupil to:

- know what he is doing
- understand the effects of what he is doing
- speculate why – the hardest task
- speculate on the outcome – for himself now and as the year goes by
- ask himself if he wants to change and whether he can

The whole-group work should help all pupils ask these questions of themselves, and the group exploration should especially help the at-risk or active bully. It will need to be supplemented by very carefully and sensitively handled one-to-one discussion in the hope of gaining further trust and assisting further self-understanding. There should also be attempts to answer the underlying question: 'What needs is this behaviour illegitimately meeting?' Then some attempt must be made to help the bully meet those needs in a more positive, pleasing and self-enhancing way. Can the tutor enable the 'bully' to make school more rewarding?

The frequent issue of bullying, both for aggressor and victim, is another example of how a tutor can complement on-the-spot reaction by a deeper enabling and empowering of the pupil.

## Summing up

The key aspects of these explorations are obvious: the tutor can take the initiative by finding ways of enabling group and individuals to find ways to an understanding of self and others, and of social pressures – and through that to deciding to, and being able to, take control of self.

Much of tutoring is signalling the ordinary choices made in school as a paradigm of life. The mutually respecting group led by the sensitive but intellectually clear tutor will move from the present to the presented, from the small to the large, and from the particular to the general.

Overall, the tutor will enable the members of the group to develop their own ideas and strategies. Exhortations will fade away as the pupil is enabled to find those strategies. This enabling cannot be left to the serendipity of daily happenings; it has to be planned. This is the 'curriculum' aspect of pastoral care in general and within that, tutoring. It is out of that planning that the 'tutorial programme' is devised – the subject of our next chapter.

# 5 The tutorial programme

## Tutoring and the curriculum

Whatever the overall curriculum plan for personal-social development – and even when this includes specific courses – there is a
major *tutorial* task in the whole-group tutorial programme. Even
with the most vigorous presentation of certain topics in the range
of standard school courses (e.g. science, English and humanities)
and even when there are specifically designed PSHE courses, there
remains a sequence of 'topics' and activities that embody the
intended learning outcomes for personal-social development that
are best handled by the tutors in the tutorial programme. Some use
the term 'active tutorial work' for this; others call it the 'pastoral
curriculum'. Whatever the whole-school plan, tutors need a programme to bring together the personal-social aspects of the
curriculum with their special holistic knowledge of the individual
tutee's overall development and the group work of the tutor
group.

A 1989 government committee of enquiry into discipline in
schools summed up the basic minimum of a tutorial programme
as:

> Tutor periods are valuable opportunities to carry out pastoral
> work. They can be used to teach study skills or to deliver part of
> the school's PSE programme. We have emphasised form tutors'
> central role in effective pastoral systems earlier in this chapter. A
> structured programme of activities should help to develop the
> relationship between tutors and their groups. We recommend
> that secondary headteachers and teachers should identify clear
> aims for the use of tutorial time, and that these aims should
> include reinforcing the school's behaviour policy.
>
> (DES/Welsh Office, 1989, para 105)

Pastoral care has moved gradually from a reactive to a proactive approach. Positive arguments have been put forward for the value of the curriculum content of tutorial periods as the emphasis shifted from only helping individuals to providing more whole-group work. Essentially, the argument is that pastoral care is based on personal growth. The growing adolescent needs to develop a range of concepts, attitudes, facts and skills if she is to make best use of school, establish her own sense of self, move towards a moral understanding, build a range of social relationships, be prepared to contribute to community life, and focus on making vocational choices.

To meet these needs, we have to complement and lay foundations for individual pastoral care through ensuring parts of the overall curriculum specifically assist these aspects of a pupil's growth. That is to say, elements of the whole-school curriculum must have primarily a pastoral function, which can be called 'the pastoral curriculum'.

Without curriculum foundations, guidance is inevitably weak. For example, how can a tutor help a pupil cope better with her work if that pupil has no grasp of study skills? How can a careers officer help a pupil decide what he wants to be when that pupil doesn't know what there is to be?

Obviously, many subjects include aspects in their curriculum designed to help pupils' personal growth: one can point to some passages in literature or to elements of biology. But in many schools, these aspects remain uncoordinated and tend to be taught separately in well-meaning but isolated departments. The term 'pastoral curriculum', first used in 1980 (Marland, 1980), implies the school should adopt a whole-school approach and work out detailed curriculum schemes, which will be implemented in a planned way in agreed subjects and group tutorial sessions. Thus, aspects of study skills can be taught in the tutorial programme, and in science, English, home economics, design & technology, and humanities.

Different terms are used for this aspect of a school's work. In many schools, it is called 'personal–social development'; in some 'personal and social education (PSE)' or, adding in health, PSHE; and in others the Ofsted term 'spiritual, moral, social and cultural education (SMSC)'. The overall concept is deeply embedded in the overarching requirements of the curriculum legislation, and scrutinized in Ofsted inspections as SMSC. The division of responsibility between the different delivery routes varies. These routes are:

- the general National Curriculum-derived courses
- specific personal-social development courses
- the communal life of the school
- residential experience, when possible
- the whole-school environment, and
- the tutorial programme

Many schools find the overall planning and division into delivery routes difficult. Some place too much emphasis on specific courses, and underplay the value of the tutor's unique overall knowledge of the tutees. Others leave too much to tutors. The 1995/96 annual report of Her Majesty's Chief Inspector of Schools commented:

Much work in the areas of spiritual, moral, social and cultural education, including health education, falls within personal and social education (PSE). In about four in ten schools, PSE is well planned and taught. In one in four schools, provision is poor. Weaknesses often occur when the programme is taught by form tutors, who lack sufficient knowledge and teaching skills in the more sensitive areas of sex and drugs education. In addition, tutor periods are usually too short to deal with important and complex issues. In general, personal and social education is more successful when it is taught by a specialist team in timetabled time.

(Ofsted, 1997)

The value of an all-embracing approach to pastoral care is hinted at in a section on sixth forms, where the Chief Inspector added:

Most schools create a positive ethos in their sixth forms. Students value the orderly, supportive community with which they have become familiar. They appreciate what they regard as a good balance between demands for work and behaviour of a high standard and opportunities for exercising independence and initiative.

(Ofsted, 1997)

By 2004, the Chief Inspector was reporting that PSHE programmes were effective in three fifths of schools but poor in one in twelve, adding that such programmes improve 'when there is a greater use of specialist teachers' (Ofsted, 2004).

Fears that the National Curriculum has eroded the teaching of personal and social education persist, although the Qualifications and Curriculum Authority (QCA) documents have deepened and widened the expectation on personal development. These reflected the growing concern for pupils' personal and social development, originally highlighted in 1997 by the School Curriculum and Assessment Authority (SCAA) discussion documents on moral education and values, and the setting up by SCAA of a National Forum for Values in Education and the Community. One of the Forum's aims was to make recommendations on how schools might be supported in making their contribution to pupils' spiritual, moral, social and cultural development – in effect, how to fulfil the requirements of Section 1(2) of the Education Reform Act 1988 (HMSO, 1988).

While it is true that all aspects of a school and its whole curriculum should contribute to personal and social development, there needs to be a specific whole-school policy ('the pastoral curriculum') listing all those concepts, attitudes, facts and skills necessary for personal and social growth. This may be in a single curriculum policy or in a number of related ones. Some schools use the Ofsted linking of spiritual, moral, social and cultural; others use the older PSE, or include Health (PSHE). Sometimes these are known as the 'cross-curricular themes' of the National Curriculum.

The Venn diagram opposite can help a tutor to think of the interrelationship between pastoral care and the curriculum.

The circle on the left is the curriculum as a whole, which will be divided into different courses in different schools. Most National Curriculum 'subjects' will appear as separate courses, though there will be variations, especially in Key Stage Three (KS3), and there is

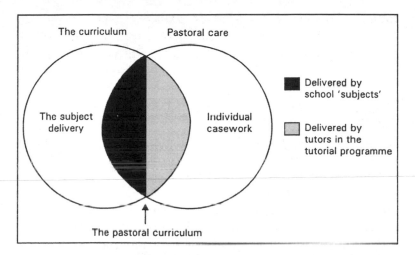

Figure 3  The interrelationship between pastoral care and the curriculum

no legal requirement that a school's courses should be coterminous with the subject planning divisions of the National Curriculum. Indeed, central government stated this very clearly in 2003:

> Whilst the National Curriculum is specified in terms of separate subjects, schools are not required to teach the subjects discretely. The way teaching is timetabled and how lessons are described and organised is not prescribed and it is for each school to decide the organising structures to use.
>
> (DfES, 2003c, p. 5)

Thus the 'courses' and the tutorial periods can be devised as the school thinks best.

In the range of courses, most schools have some specific PSHE-type courses. Some schools have broad integrated courses, but others have more closely focused ones, with teachers specializing in a rotation of courses, e.g. on study skills, on interpersonal relations, on health.

In the diagram: the circle on the right is all aspects of pastoral care. The shaded intersection is those aspects of the curriculum required primarily and centrally for pastoral care: the *pastoral curriculum*. Some parts of that curriculum will be taught through the subjects and courses on the school timetable. However, the tutorial sessions, which we have described in Chapter 1 as 'the integrative centre' of the curriculum, also have a 'delivery role' in the whole-school curriculum. Some specific parts will be the responsibility of tutors: the *tutorial programme*. Ideally, these aspects of the pastoral curriculum should be clearly defined and located for 'delivery' up the years, and across the school's teaching and tutorial organization.

The tutorial programme, therefore, is the planned sequence of aspects of the pastoral curriculum which are agreed to be the responsibility of the tutor, and closely related to his central task of enabling the pupil to understand herself and society. Some schools use the term 'the pastoral curriculum' for this, whereas we prefer to use that term for *all* aspects of the curriculum that relate to personal and social growth. (For analyses of the pastoral curriculum, see Bulman and Jenkins, 1988; Marland, 1980; and the two key SCAA booklets of 1996 and 1997.)

Some aspects of the overall pastoral curriculum will be both subject syllabuses and the tutorial programme. For example, individual guidance and support depend on facts, understanding and skills. But there are times across the curriculum when facts and concepts are paramount and self-reflection less important – although one never wholly abandons the other. In tutorial work, it is helpful to see the relationship of knowledge about self and personal skills on the one hand and facts and concepts on the other as interrelated – as in the diagram below:

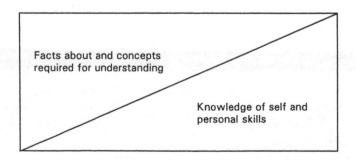

Figure 4    The interrelationship of self-understanding and objective facts

This diagram suggests that only rarely can self-understanding be explored without some objective facts, and conversely it is impossible to consider facts objectively without some feeling for self-understanding. However, the balance varies. Of course, the subject syllabus part of the curriculum is presumed to lie towards the left of the diagram, and the tutorial towards the right. Both are necessary and one cannot do without the other.

It is interesting to note the difference in learning context between the two and the implications for the experiences of the pupils.

- In subject periods, the *personal* aspect of a topic is usually less the focus than its place in the overall structure of the subject.
- In tutorial periods, the context is one in which family and home background, previous educational history, and the whole pattern of study over the week should all be well known to the tutor. The tutor is the main contact with home; has the greatest disciplinary influence; probably has the most intimate relationship; and above all has the broadest responsibility for the pupil's personal, educational and vocational guidance. Topics therefore have a different flavour, impact and response in a tutorial period. For example, the tutorial context for aspects of learning skills has a generalizing possibility less easy in a subject; discussion about relationships at home has a more personal context from the tutor's knowledge of parents and guardians; aspects of sexuality more readily related to the emotional than the biological; anti-racism is looked at through known personal incidents rather than just through language and literature.

There is a sense in which the tutorial programme merges with subject teaching, when a content of some form is to be learned, and individual guidance given, and when the task is to respond to the pupil's personal needs. A tutorial period has to be structured in some ways like any lesson, but often more flexibility is required as the main content is the pupils themselves and what is, or could be, happening to them.

A reciprocal relationship exists between the academic subjects and the pastoral curriculum or personal and social education. HMI put it interestingly and powerfully when it reported, some years ago now, on personal and social education:

The fostering of personal and social development is a means as well as an end of education. For effective learning to occur schools have to develop a moral framework acceptable to parents, teachers and pupils within which initiative, responsibility and sound relationships can flourish. Equally, the promotion of knowledge, understanding and related competencies should contribute to the development in pupils of relevant personal, social and moral characteristics.

(HMI, 1989, p. 2)

The PSHE aspect of the National Curriculum can be seen as deriving from the generic description of pastoral care – 'personal, educational, and vocational guidance'. While many schools have well-developed curriculum policies and overall tutorial plans, you may be working in a school which has not been able to achieve these aims. A more recent report by the Chief Inspector commented on the PSHE curriculum that 'the most effective teaching is by teachers with a special interest and expertise in the subject' (Ofsted, 2003).

The ideal tutorial programme should be a subset of the overall pastoral curriculum. If this has not been possible in your school, you still need as a tutor to have a tutorial programme which offers an overarching scheme and materials for your whole-group tutoring.

## The uses of source material

Tutorial work cannot be derived entirely from the thoughts of tutor and pupil or the actions and experiences of the group members. It needs to draw on wider source materials for a variety of purposes:

- to set out information
- to distance or objectify what is being discussed
- to evoke with the vividness of art a mood or situation
- to provide case studies of situations beyond those experienced directly by the members of the group

From one point of view, the art of group tutoring is that of taking pupils away from themselves to consider aspects of

relationships and then bringing them back to relate their perceptions of the other to themselves. Neither extreme is sufficient:
group tutorial work cannot focus only on the pupils themselves the
whole time. Conversely, it cannot be looking 'out there' and away
from the pupils for too long.

Moving from the immediate self to the more objective distant
example and back again widens pupils' appreciation of what people
are like – and at the same time gives them deeper insight into
themselves. To some extent, this is the content of many literature
lessons. However, in such a lesson the text is there for its own sake
and the search within oneself for points of contact is to help
construct a fuller meaning of the literary work. In the tutorial
session, the teacher's art is reversed: the extension and reverbera-
tions of the text are there to help one pupil review himself and
another to reconstruct her view of herself.

The kinds of source material which can be used include:
photographs, cartoons, drawings, paintings, biography and auto-
biography, literature, argumentative writing, statistics, and factual
studies.

These can be presented in a variety of formats: printed text,
white board, powerpoint, wall displays, projected slides, work
sheets, tutor/pupil readings, computer programmes, audio tapes
and discs, video tapes and films, and separately printed photographs.

They can be grouped in several ways, such as by content or use.
The important point is that the tutor has to be willing to deploy a
full range of material so the tutorial group can explore a variety of
content and presentation. Try, also, to avoid a monotonous pattern
of the same sequence: stimulus, discussion, writing.

Tutors with different subject backgrounds will be more familiar
with some formats than others. An English teacher may not be
used to slides; a technology teacher may not have used much text.
However, there is nothing beyond the teacher's ordinary skill in
weaving any of these forms into a tutorial session, and tutors should
be encouraged to try all of them.

The different kinds of material have specific characteristic qualities; literature, statistics, visual images and factual analysis explore
and evoke reality in various ways. All are useful in tutorial work,
but they demand consciously different approaches.

Tutors unused to discussing literature need not feel daunted by the evocation of people in particular situations. It is often helpful to read such a passage aloud to the group, as the tutor's reading brings the characters and atmosphere to life. Sometimes a member of the group can be asked to read an extract, but it will often be wise to ask in advance so that the pupil can prepare the passage. The point of using extracts is not as a reading exercise; the aim must be to focus on the theme and the pupil's experience and review of him- or herself.

In general, with fiction pupils tend to be good at recalling a story sequence, naming people and locating the events in places. However, they are often far less comfortable recalling qualitative aspects, and have even more trouble deducing the author's intentions or the extract's theme. Indeed, the distinction between 'story' and 'theme' can be very difficult for most pupils. 'It is about . . .' will lead them more often into re-telling plot than exploring theme.

Real-life descriptions or dialogues from autobiographies or news stories can powerfully evoke situations which ring true to the pupils and clearly relate to their own understanding, but at the same time give them a fresh perspective.

Audio cassettes, though not often used, can be remarkably effective, concentrating on the experience of the words, which can be lost in the visual fascination of video. Still photographs allow the tutees to concentrate on the expressions on people's faces and thus deepen their understanding of the expressions of others. In questions and discussions, the aim should be to help the tutorial group members to participate in the thoughts and feelings of the speakers, but at the same time to look at those experiences objectively:

- what is this person feeling and why?
- how has she come to make this decision?
- what would be the outcome if . . . ?

The special value of literature, biography, the media and photographs is their power to involve the pupil. The special value of objective analysis is the complementary one of allowing breadth of consideration. The pupil is helped to stand back from considering *this* person or *that* moment and to ponder more generally on how people appear to be. For example, an obvious part of all tutorial work is to discuss gender: what is it to be a girl or boy? This could hardly be considered without using the vividness of art, but also the perspective of the social scientist and psychologist.

In every example, tutors should encourage pupils to be clear about the kind of material they are considering and, albeit briefly, the provenance. For example, photographs are not 'real life' but someone's deliberate selection of viewpoint:

- why was *this* photographed?
- why *this* angle?
- why is the photograph cropped as it is?
- why did the editor choose it?

Using newspaper clippings, video and audio recordings can help pupils get used to 'critiquing' material and understanding how the media works. This should be covered in the National Curriculum requirements for English at Key Stages 3 and 4. However, the tutor should not feel daunted by any lack of specialized knowledge. An adult, common-sense approach is sufficient to help pupils ask and provide answers to such questions as:

- to what extent can we trust this newspaper account?
- could the accident victim's relatives have really said this?
- how do 'real' statements differ from extracts from fictional stories?

Many tutorial teams devise their own programmes of materials and duplicate them in-house; others use published material. Experience in many schools shows that when tutors are first given printed material to use in tutor groups, many feel tied to it in a passive way that they would consider quite inappropriate for learning material in their own specialist subject. This is not surprising since subject teachers are trained to use their own subject matter with confidence and therefore with flexibility. Many tutors do not have the same confidence but will find it gradually easier as they become more experienced with whole-group tutorial work. The resources provided for such work are meant to facilitate it rather than dominate it. The real 'programme' is the learning aims behind the material. In no school activity should the work be limited to or by the material available.

Even those tutors in schools using fully worked-out schemes will, of course, want to use a variety of other material, such as: school events, incidents from pupils' lives, anniversaries and religious festivals, and topics related to the pupils in the class, such as a new admission or a family illness. While it would be unwise to let a tutor group move from one recent incident to another, responding only to events, it would be entirely against the experiential learning of a tutor group not to focus on what is happening to members here and now. Sometimes, other relevant themes can be brought into a scheme or supplementary material introduced to provide a local context.

Much tutorial work can have ambitions beyond the material available, and tutors can improvise too extensively. In such groups, anecdote, opinion and garrulous talk about not very much can lead to shallowness. Often the boredom and emptiness of listening is replaced by the boredom of toying with a worksheet that demands action but no thought. Successful group tutoring is based on the flexible use of a wide range of source material to inform, evoke, stimulate and prompt.

An interesting contrast is the use made of a piece of literature or drama video about, say, bullying in a tutor session and in an English lesson. The English teacher would ask for memories and speculation about bullying as part of the lesson. However, such personal experiences would be evoked primarily to help pupils react to and make sense of the drama. Conversely, the tutor is using the drama to help pupils make sense of their own experience.

Of course, this exaggerates the polarity: all reading and watching drama helps the reader or audience consider their own human predicament. As Doris Lessing says of one of her characters:

> She therefore got out of bed, and went into the living room, and knelt in front of the bookcase. Books. Words. There must surely be some pattern of words which would neatly and safely cage what she felt – isolate her emotions so that she could look at them from outside . . . And so she knelt in front of the bookcase, in driving need of the right arrangement of words . . . with the craving thought, what does this say about my life?
>
> (Doris Lessing, *A Proper Marriage*, MacGibbon & Kee, 1965)

However, from the presentational point of view, the tutor can use this polarity: she must focus the introduction, the purpose and the follow-up in terms of enabling the pupils the better to understand situations so that they can control themselves and the situation better. The art is there primarily to help them take a better grip on themselves and their surroundings.

## The programme and the experience

Over the year, there should be a reciprocal relationship between individual and whole-group tutorial programme work, with one prompting and illuminating the other.

If pupils are to objectivize their behaviour, they need to be able to stand outside, as it were, and look on as a spectator. This can be helped by providing data on how others behave. For example, take school attendance. There are ample statistics on attendance in one's own school and nationally against which to set a single tutor group's pattern of attendance, and against which each pupil can consider herself. The issue is not so much the number of absences as the pattern of absence, e.g. how absence is connected to what is on the timetable, the subject, the time of day, being taught by a particular teacher. Speculating about cause and effect in the behaviour of others can also help to an analysis of self.

Discussions with tutees can be supplemented by questionnaires, and can range beyond the specific issue of attendance to a consideration of the importance of education and the positive aspects of school. Susan Hallam, in *Improving School Attendance* (Heinemann School Management series, 1996, p. 25) suggests possible starting points:

- why do we have schools?
- why do you come to school?
- do all children attend school every day?
- why do you think that some don't attend?
- do some pupils skip particular lessons?
- why do you think that they do?

The discussions, she adds, can raise such issues as:

- general reasons why pupils do not attend school
- particular lessons that are disliked – and why
- particular teachers who are disliked – and why
- difficulties with friends at school
- difficulties at home

Another example is to ask a tutor group of 12- and 13-year-olds to consider the facts about absence from school and smoking habits based on a large survey of children of the same age:

## Numbers (percentages) of absences related to children's smoking

| smoked: | never | sometimes | regularly |
|---------|-------|-----------|-----------|
| boys | 181/877 (21%) | 109/486 (22%) | 21/45 (47%) |
| girls | 157/947 (17%) | 117/487 (24%) | 17/43 (40%) |

(Charlton and Blair, 1989, p. 91)

The tutor can raise such questions as:

- why are regular smokers absent from school more often than other children?
- could it be chance, an unrelated correlation?
- does the smoking lead to absence, perhaps through ill health?
- does lack of success at and interest in school lead to absence, and the absence itself lead to smoking?
- as parental smoking appears to lead to less good health in children, does early ill health lead to less success in school, and so to more absence?

Discussing these hypotheses and exploring and interpreting the facts are well within the ideas and skills of almost all second-year secondary tutor groups. Indeed, give or take a few points of vocabulary and syntax, their arguments are likely to be as thoughtful, shrewd and relevant as those of the researchers:

Our findings suggest that children who smoke and whose parents smoke are more likely to be absent from school for minor ailments. Their schoolwork would then suffer and they might be underachievers because of their smoking and their families' smoking rather than smokers because of their under-achievement. A mother's smoking during pregnancy, while breast feeding, and during a child's early infancy can cause considerable health risks to the child long before that child has started smoking. If the child thus starts school already with an increased risk of absence, failure to keep up with his or her peers could begin immediately, paving the way for under-achievement and a negative attitude to school early in his or her educational career and leading to an increased risk of smoking.

(op. cit., pp. 91–2)

On the one hand, a major pressure on young people is to conform to the tutor group – the pressure of the peer group. On the other hand, most (though not all) young people want to 'be themselves'. Facts and understanding are required to facilitate this independence. The following matrix is an attempt to define the relationships:

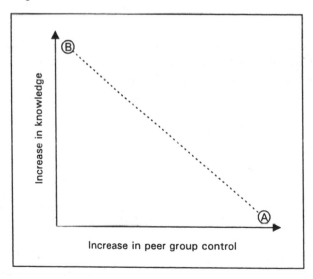

Figure 5    A pupil at A is under the maximum control of the peer group and has little knowledge to achieve independence. However, a pupil at B is less controlled by the peer group and has a large knowledge base.

This process of pupils comparing an analysis of their own behaviour with figures from other studies can be used most profitably. For example, a year 8 tutor group considered their watching of television. Each pupil estimated her or his own pattern of TV viewing over one week. The tutor then asked the pupils to keep a diary for the week ahead of their actual figure of viewing for each night. The following week's tutorial session focused on the tabulation of the previously filed expectation against the reality. National viewing figures were then compared as an external reference.

## Conclusion

As a designated tutor, you have the right to expect:

- an overall brief on the role of the tutor
- an outline of the school's general approach to SMSC, its pastoral curriculum or PSHE programme
- a more detailed description of the content of the tutorial responsibility
- pupil learning material within and exemplifying that – this is a tutorial programme

A tutorial programme is essential for every school – and if your school does not have a detailed tutorial programme, you will need to devise one for yourself, as part of the year or house team.

# 6 Relating to families

## Introduction

A school owes a duty to the families of its pupils. Families look to us not only to teach their children, but to relate to them as families. It has become clearer than ever that when home and school work together, the pupil has a better chance of success, families are more content and teachers enjoy greater professional satisfaction (see Shah, 2001, for an overview).

This approach has informed a swathe of recent educational and social welfare legislation. For example, it underpins the original requirements for providing for special educational needs in the Education Act 1993, with its *Code of Practice* (DfEE, 1994) expecting 'the greatest possible degree of partnership' between parents, their children, the school, LEA and other relevant agencies. It is also a central part of the legislation and guidance to meet the wider welfare and needs of children and their families set out in the Children Act 1989, and developed in the Government's *Every Child Matters* strategy (DfES, 2003/4) and new Children Bill (TSO, 2004). The strategy's overall aim is to 'ensure that every child gets personalised learning, care and support' (DfES, 2004), with schools working in closer partnership with other child-related services through, for example, Children's Trusts.

Schools, therefore, are increasingly looking for ways to form positive and active partnerships with parents. They are also becoming more involved with those other social and health service agencies, both statutory and voluntary, which engage with families in the welfare interests of children and young people.

The re-positioning of schools in this personal and social landscape – and, by implication, in the territory for tutoring responsibilities – is highlighted by two comments. The first is from the 1989 government committee of enquiry into discipline, chaired by Lord Elton:

We draw attention to evidence indicating that the most effective schools tend to be those with the best relationships with parents. We urge heads and teachers to ensure that they keep parents well informed, that their schools provide a welcoming atmosphere which encourages parents to become involved, and that parents are not only told when their children are in trouble but when they have behaved particularly well.

(DES/Welsh Office, 1989, p. 14)

The second comes from guidance for schools from the children's mental health charity Young Minds:

The teacher is in a central position to promote the mental health of his or her students, through establishing clear rules, providing encouragement and setting a good example. The teacher can also do a great deal to help those with problems through good management, offering the chance to talk, listening, noticing signs of difficulties and bringing in extra help from within and outside the school when necessary.

(Young Minds, 1996, p. 42)

All this puts a considerable emphasis on the tutorial role. Yet, despite numerous statements from the DfES and the school inspection agency Ofsted about the value of working with parents, there are many more complaints from families about poor communication than there are criticizing teachers. Indeed, after decades of very little attention having been given by central government or in teacher training to the professional knowledge and skills required for relating to parents and carers, since 2002 there has been a key component in the QTS Standards of Initial Teacher Training, which we have quoted on pages 12–14, and since September 2003 there has been the following formal wording in the requirement for the Induction Standards, which 'build on that QTS Standard': 'Liaise effectively with parents or carers on pupils' progress and achievements.' (Teacher Training Agency, 2003a, p. 18)

Although relating to parents and carers is a responsibility for all members of the school's staff, and year heads have a special role, it is a key part of the form tutor's role and is very important for his or her work. Indeed, the form tutor is in most cases the coordinator of the school's liaison with homes. The tutor has the prime responsibility for a school's relations with families, in collaboration with attendance officers and support staff, and this chapter addresses this task.

## Difficulties

Even experienced teachers, sometimes to their surprise, feel considerable difficulty in working with parents. They might take some comfort from knowing how widespread this lack of confidence is. Indeed, we have hard figures from HMI/Ofsted studies of how new teachers feel about their preparation. In 1987, 'fewer than two in ten new teachers felt well prepared to liaise with parents and others in the community' (HMI, 1988). Five years later, in 1992, the situation had not improved: only 16 per cent of new teachers felt well prepared 'to meet parents and report to them' (Ofsted, 1993).

More recently, Ofsted reports that there has been a growing awareness by schools of the need to ease newly qualified teachers (NQTs) into taking on pastoral tasks:

> As [NQTs] grew in confidence and experience, many secondary schools eased the NQTs into increased pastoral responsibilities and duties, often by shadowing a form tutor in preparation for the role. Most NQTs welcomed these extra responsibilities.
>
> (Ofsted, 2001)

It is not enough to assume that teachers will take working with parents in their stride, especially as the hours spent with pupils in classes and with other teachers in planning and discussion take up so much time. In even the keenest teacher's year, there will only be a tiny fraction of that time working with parents. You can be an experienced teacher but remain inexperienced working with pupils' families. How, then, can a tutor move forward realistically?

## Getting to know the family

The better you know a particular family's pattern, the better you will be able to relate to that family. Getting to know a family requires an open mind. We all have stereotypical views of the family so that we often jump to wrong conclusions. It is easy to make assumptions about the pattern of family life on the basis of a few snippets of information that prove to be quite erroneous. For example, the Government Household Survey for 1994 reports that only one in four children in school comes from a traditional two-parent nuclear family. So the first step is to avoid guesswork. Schools should ensure they have on file basic family information about every pupil.

This is best done not only by a questionnaire but by a complementary 'reception interview' during which important, and sometimes sensitive, information can be asked for, such as:

- the adults caring for the pupils
- their relationship to the pupil and (if more than one) to each other
- the names and titles by which they wish to be known
- if the pupil's two biological parents are not the present caring adults, how and when did the absent parent(s) leave, and what is the present relationship with the pupil
- the occupations of the caring adults
- their correct addresses and telephone numbers of home and work
- any siblings' names, ages and present education or occupation
- the ethnicity of family members
- the languages spoken
- the housing situation (in broad terms)

Those teachers who have often interviewed families have nearly always found that families are anxious to speak about themselves. The school is a privileged recipient as it enters the partnership of assisting with the education of the young person.

Whether your tutor group is new to the school or you are taking over an established group, it is well worth looking through those files to back up the bald details of the register. You will not want to make simple, but embarrassing or upsetting, slips such as wrong names, including dead parents, or misunderstanding relationships. You may therefore like to prepare a personal checklist. At the least, families deserve the courtesy of correct names: if your tutee is called John Frazer and his parents are Mary Jones and James Frazer, they should not be written to as Mr and Mrs Frazer! Similarly, Islamic family name patterns should be understood and used correctly.

## Making first contact

Having done your homework, a general introductory letter is a welcome and practical first step. This is not often done, but much appreciated when it is. This may not be needed if your school includes tutors' names in circular letters. Even so, a letter to the parents of your tutees to introduce yourself, say what you hope to achieve, and how you can best be contacted, can be very useful. How much better that your first communication should be warm, helpful, and pleasant rather than a query about absence! A sample letter – from a fictitious school – follows:

To the families of 9Q

Dear Parents or Guardians,

I know that after two years of working with him the pupils of 9Q and their parents and guardians were very sad that Mr Cheshire retired at the end of last year. You will be pleased to know that he and his wife are happily settled in their new home – and he seems to be as active in the community as ever!

May I introduce myself as your daughter's/son's new Tutor. I have been at the school for many years now and I know the pupils of this group rather well as I taught my subject, Mathematics, to them last year (and I shall continue teaching them this year also). Mr Cheshire has briefed me very thoroughly, and I am familiar with each of the pupil's records and her or his work last year.

I look forward to getting to know you also. I shall read the pupil's *Diaries* every Thursday during the morning, and I shall look out for your comments. Please keep in touch with me. You can always write a brief note in the *Diary* or send in a separate letter. In particular, please let me know if for any reason your son or daughter is unable to be at school.

If you want to speak with me on the phone, please ask for the Lower-School staffroom. Of course, I teach most of the periods and if I am not available please leave a message in the Lower-School office, and I shall try to get back to you as soon as possible.

I shall be looking at all the work of the pupils in my group, and especially concentrating this year on further developing their study skills – remembering that they start their two-year study course next year. We shall also be starting work towards their option choices. This is very important, not only so that they choose the best subjects to add to the national curriculum itself, but also because this task of considering and choosing is in itself important to every pupil's personal and intellectual growth. The first meeting to discuss this will be on October 6$^{th}$ and I'll send you the details later.

I am looking forward to the year's work with my new Tutor Group, and I think that they will do very well.

Best wishes,

Yours sincerely,

Brenda Casey
Tutor of 9Q

## Keeping in touch

From then on, the tutor will want to keep each pupil's family as well informed as possible. Most schools have some form of booklet which is used for regular exchanges of facts – homework assignments, absences, special arrangements, and notes on good work or difficulties. In recent years, many have been carefully redesigned to encourage tutor–family interchange.

The early pages of this termly booklet provide pupils' homes with the names of the key teachers in the school, and a page of advice to parents or carers, translated into the main languages used by the families whose children attend the school.

- subject teachers are expected to ensure that the defined homework assignment is copied into the appropriate space
- families are expected to check that this tallies with the homework timetable set out earlier
- all teachers are expected to enter comments and points of interest
- tutors are expected to oversee this communication flow, the lynchpin of which is the exchange of comments between tutor and home

For such a scheme to work, the whole school has to support it and work at the details. For example, every subject teacher must be meticulous about ensuring that homework assignments are noted, and praise or criticism entered. The scheme helps the tutor to build up a picture of the pupil across the curriculum and in the school as a whole. But for the family, it is their main link with the school and they will see it primarily as a way to hear from and speak to you as a tutor. It therefore repays care. If you are tutoring in a school without such a booklet, you will find both the cross-school picture and the home-school link harder to build up – to have to make every small point in the form of a letter is more laborious and can be artificial. One option is to devise a simple form of quick messages – see page 102. Such a slip can be used easily and makes up in part for the lack of a booklet.

## Letters

There are times when a full letter is required, especially when a tutor sees significant developments, achievements, or problems, or examples of worrying bad behaviour. In some schools it is the practice for only the senior middle-management pastoral staff or year heads to write full letters. However, the tutor's letter is always very helpful. Two obvious difficulties arise: lack of time and shortage of clerical facilities even after the 2003 work-load changes. Another less often mentioned one is how rarely teachers have occasion to write professionally for adult readers. We tend to be abrupt, use needlessly 'official' or even officious language, and strangely cold: 'I have to tell you . . .' 'It has come

**WAVERLEY SCHOOL**
Station Road Bishop Norton Lancashire LA4 6PL

FROM MS GRACE, TUTOR OF 2GH

Date:......................

To the parents or guardians of:................................

Please excuse this quick note, but I thought you would want to
know at once that:

I should be grateful if you could contact me by a note or phone
to let me know your reactions as soon as possible.

signed:............................

Figure 6    A sample proforma note from a tutor

to our attention that your son/daughter . . .' 'I must insist . . .' 'It is school policy that . . .'.

The passive is too frequently used in sentences which evade the point: 'It has become clear that . . .'. Often, the writer so suppresses his own voice that he sounds like a clerk working mechanically to the instructions of superiors. Conversely, as in speaking, it is easy to let indignation or strength of feeling lead to insulting remarks. One pupil's father complained that his son's tutor has said of a matter of option choice over which tutor and father disagreed: 'What a pity you've chosen that when Jason is so capable. Parents are usually more caring in these matters.'

We advise, therefore, that letters should as far as possible be phrased with warmth, courtesy and hope. Officialese should be banished. Use a suitable opening paragraph which pick up the relationship where it was last left, as adults do in other contexts, for example:

Dear Mrs Brown,
I was glad to hear that your youngest daughter has settled so well into her junior school. You must be very pleased. When we last spoke, I promised to let you know how John seems to be managing the range of preparation for GCSE. Although there are still some difficulties, you will be pleased to hear . . .

## Tutor-group family meetings

Tutor-group parents' meetings are used successfully in many schools: the tutor invites parents to meet each other and him. This is particularly useful early in the life of a group. An invitation, giving the expected time of ending and the main purpose, is much appreciated:

To the parents and guardians of pupils of 10J

Dear Guardians and Parents,

As I promised you when I wrote to introduce myself at the start of the year, I have arranged for a meeting of the families of the students in my Tutor Group:

*Wednesday, 16th October, 6:30 p.m.*

The main purpose is for parents and guardians to be able to meet me and the new Head of Year, Miss Oakes. Please bring your daughter or son if you wish. There will be coffee and biscuits at 6:30pm, and some members of the Tutor Group will be here in advance to greet you and introduce you to others.

At about 7.00 pm Miss Oakes and I will give a very short description of the special features this term, with particular reference to assessment in relation to the National Curriculum and progress towards GCSE. This will last only some twenty minutes, and then will we shall be happy to answer questions about general matters until 8.00pm. I promise that no one need stay after that, though we should both be happy to speak to families individually about personal queries if you would like to stay.

There will be a display in the room of the group work we have been doing in tutorial sessions, which I hope will interest you.

We look forward to seeing you.

Best wishes,

Yours sincerely,

Harry J. Counter
Tutor of 10J

You will need to debate whether to meet in the usual tutor-group room or in a larger and less desk-filled venue; both have advantages. A cup of tea or coffee can help get things going. Allow a little time for introductions and informal talk before starting the meeting. Cover routine points, how the group is settling in, and the main needs of the group. Then invite families to ask questions about any aspect of the school and how it works. The tutor should note down and promise to follow up any problems, however small.

Be relaxed but precise – resisting the temptation to be too defens-
ive about the school. Parents prefer, and deserve, honesty about
difficulties.

Tutor-group parent sessions can have a variety of valuable
focuses: an induction session for a new group, an end-of-year
review, Year 10 options, GCSE preparation. David Kibble sums
up his use of a session on study skills for the parents of Year Eleven
pupils as follows:

> In discussion the parents said how valuable it had been to learn
> about revision techniques. Many realised how inefficient pupils
> might be. One parent commented that his own son had adopted
> some of the techniques of study and revision following the
> pupils' study skills course and now felt himself to be much
> more efficient. The father was able to see why. Here was an
> excellent example of the true partnership of school and parent I
> mentioned earlier. Other parents felt that sharing experiences
> and ideas had been the most valuable part of the evening. They
> felt that they were more able to understand the pressure on their
> children and the subsequent 'distancing' and bad temper of some
> of their sons and daughters.
>
> (Kibble, 1988, p. 43)

Obviously, such events can be organized for a whole year group,
but from time to time special tutor-group meetings are well
worthwhile.

## The family and the tutor programme

Tutors should create an atmosphere in which their pupils know
that their homes are respected and there is mutual trust. As in any
family, there will be times when the Tutor must make clear to a
pupil that something – perhaps an uncharacteristic show of bad
behaviour – will not be passed over but will also not be passed on.

The whole-group tutorial programme should consciously address the matter of family care and responsibility. This is another
example of relating pastoral casework to the pastoral curriculum.
As in the earlier discussion of homework, which highlighted
the need to consider home-school information and planning (see

pages 60–62), the following hand-out addresses the relationship directly:

## School and Home

### School and Home – how are they getting on?

Now that you've been in your first year for a while, you've got to know the school, and people in school have got to know you.

And what about the folks at home?

Have they got to know about school? Has school got to know about them?

### A quiz for parents/guardians

How many of these questions could they answer?

1. What's the name of your tutor?
2. What's your favourite lesson?
3. Which evening do you get Maths homework?
4. Which subject do you find most difficult?
5. How is a meeting arranged with someone at school?
6. What classes for adults does the school put on?

▷ Talk over with your neighbour the ones that you think your parents/guardians might not be able to answer.

Have they been given the answers at any time?

### Now it's the school's turn

How many of these questions could your tutor answer?

1. Who are the parents/guardians/adults you live with?
2. What are their names?
3. Do you have any brothers or sisters?
4. What hobbies/activities does your family enjoy?

5. *Which of your lessons are they most concerned about?*
6. *Who would be contacted in an emergency and how?*

▷ *Talk over with your neighbour the ones that you think your tutor may not be able to answer.*
   *Has s/he been given the answers at any time?*

### 'Could do better'?

▷ *Now it's your turn. You're going to write a report on school and on home, telling each of them how they could do better in doing their part toward your progress at school. You could also tell them what you think they should learn about each other.*

*Discuss your ideas in the Tutor Group before you deliver your reports to your tutor and your home.*

The tutor will want to help pupils think generally about how and why school and home work together so that individually they can make sense of their own experiences – and know what to expect. Indeed, they should be helped to know the *rights* of families in terms of the school, and understand the respective duties of school and home. The Year 9 subject choice programme is one time when the relative predominance of each member of the pupil–school–home trio can be addressed. In older years, the changing balance of responsibility is an issue of group discussion.

Ideally, questions of the family will be part of the school's wider personal-social whole-curriculum plans. In those contexts, the idea of family should be explored, for example the patterns of today, of the past and of different cultures. The social studies approach to family is objective and generalized, but should best be there to underpin tutorial work. The tutorial approach relates the under-standing of family to the pupil's consideration of self: 'Who am I?' also involves asking the additional questions 'What is my family? How do I work with it? How does my school work with my family?'

## Conclusion

No tutor will ever regret the effort, care, time and generosity she or he gives to pupils' families. There will be disappointments and misunderstandings with some families, but even here the tutor will feel happier for genuinely having tried. At a time when the profession is under great pressure and an individual teacher's duties more precisely defined than ever, it may appear ingenuous to stress the value of generosity of emotion and time to families. However, it is a privilege to be able to have a tutor's relationship with families. The rewards are very great for the pupil – and also for the tutor.

# 7 Individual casework

## Introduction

Although our theme is that the central concern of tutoring is working with and through the group, the tutor's aim is to enable the individual pupil to be more fully and truly her- or himself with an understanding of and respect for others. Neither whole-group tutoring nor one-to-one discussion can complete the task alone.

Much of the tutor's work requires individual, one-to-one 'counselling'. Pupils often need talking with and benefit from a conversation with their tutor. Such conversations – in snatched moments, after school, or in a methodically planned series of review meetings – can involve questioning, advising, exhorting, or passing on ideas or facts with which the pupil can reach their own decision. They are an essential extension of and complement to whole-group tutoring. Indeed, there is a sense in which the latter underpins or serves the former (see Chapter 5 for some examples of this reciprocity).

It is clearly a weakness of our school system that such crucial individual sessions are not budgeted for, and neither structured nor scheduled. Many problems are dealt with in passing. Tutors must therefore find their own time by a variety of devious stratagems. They usually find that individual, semi-private talks are prompted by events, too often urgent and unhappy ones, and have to be held in awkward places: the pastoral care of the corridor!

Most tutors have always been generous with their non-scheduled time, even as their workloads have increased. Paradoxically, the concept of the time-ceiling, brought in by the School Teachers' Review Body in 1987, helped because 'directed time' was a protected limit into which a school could build tutorial work. The specific budgeting of such time is a necessary corollary of encouraging full tutorial work, being both practical, because it cuts other scheduled tasks, and symbolic, because it states the reality of the need for time for tutor and tutee to meet with no competing claims. The new *National Agreement on Workload Reform* (DfES, 2003b) has given a more coherent and explicit framework for deciding what one might call issues of time-task management within the context of tutoring. The agreement also ensures 'a reasonable allocation of time in support of . . . leadership and management responsibilities' (see also *School Teachers' Review Body: Twelfth Report* DfES, 2003a).

## Pupil mobility between schools

There is a tendency in Britain to talk about schooling as if all the pupils come into the first year of a school and continue until the last – in secondary schools at least until after GCSE in Year 11. Very little advice has been given on the needs of pupils who join 'mid-course'. There was a very helpful research study by the Migration Research Unit at University College London (MRU, 2000), and a second one in 2004: *Pupil Mobility in Secondary Schools* (MRU, 2004), both funded by the Nuffield Foundation. For the first time, advice is now available from central government in a 'Guidance' booklet: *Managing Pupil Mobility* (DfES, 2003), which stresses the need for positive action by *all* the staff to help those pupils who are moving schools mid-course. There are some 'high-mobility groups': travellers, refugees, the armed forces. High-mobility situations include social deprivation and family breakup, temporary accommodation associated with rented housing, and run-down estates.

At the start of this century, 66 LEAs had data on 'a high mobility primary school', of which most had one or more schools with a mobility rate of 20 per cent. Indeed, ten LEAs had schools with a turnover of 70 per cent or more. One primary school had nine out of ten children leaving and being replaced in the course of a single year. In very many primary schools in urban areas the rate was between 10 per cent and 20 per cent. Three-quarters of all LEAs 'thought it an issue' in one or more of their secondary schools. In one very large central London school only 40 per cent of the GCSE candidates had joined the school at the start of its first year.

Although good provision for mid-course entrants requires

whole-school policies and care from the reception office and all the subject teachers, and of course especially the year head or house head, a deeply important point is that the form tutor is the key member of staff to enable the successful introduction of the mid-course entrant. His or her difficulties are great and can be acute, such as:

- family home changes
- not knowing the surrounding area
- having left behind friends and probably not knowing anyone in this school
- being unfamiliar with some of the particular routines and ways of 'getting around' here
- joining subject courses which may have covered topics not yet met, and which are difficult to connect with

Of course, as many of the 'new arrivals' are immigrants, they often bring together not only difficulties of settling into a new school but also come from a different cultural heritage and mother tongue: the combination can make her or him feel a right 'outsider', and there is a serious need for special induction courses, with very careful inclusive support from the form tutor. (The sections on ethnicity on page 25 and on refugees (see below) explore the needs of your tutees of these backgrounds.)

# Refugees

Nationally most schools do not have many children of refugee families on their rolls, but schools in a number of areas do, especially in London. The pastoral challenge is major, and however good the LEA and the school are at providing specialist support, the responsibility of the form tutor is considerable, and can be very taxing. Their families have had an increased risk of psychopathology because of traumatic life experiences, such as exposure to war and violence, and will often have suffered severe family losses. Further, their seeking asylum, moving, and attempting to settle in their host country will frequently have produced post-traumatic stress and affective disorders. To make matters worse it is often difficult for refugee families to fully access social and mental health services in some parts of this country.

Research studies in the last decades of the twentieth century have shown that:

> Particularly important are school teachers who have regular contact with the children, and who are able to identify a significant number of psychiatrically disturbed pupils.
>
> (O'Shea *et al.*, 2000, p. 190)

It is almost certain that members of staff carrying out the school's admission reception will have noted a pupil's refugee status and usually sought special external support. Indeed there are special mental health services for refugee families in some areas. The duty of the form tutor to ensure such services are kept in touch is very important. In many cases there will be translation problems for the form tutor and parents, and English as an additional language (EAL) challenges for the pupil.

Psychological studies of a range of difficulties have shown that 'of many kinds of stresses including war and natural disasters on children' they are helped by 'the buffering effect of the family' (Hodes, 2000, p. 63). Obviously, many refugee families have suffered from stress, and many 'have escaped from terrible circumstances and want and need to look forward not back'. It is clear that some families find it difficult for a variety of reasons to themselves seek mental health support. It is clear that often 'teachers can identify pupils with behavioural symptoms' and the school's referral for specialist help can therefore be very valuable.

Further, there seems to us to be a real sense in which 'the buffering effect of the family' can be extended so that the school can become part of 'the extended family', and usually the form tutor is the key link and holds the buffering role.

The tutor's especial contribution is the personal reliability and empathetic support she or he offers. A summary of the very relevant aspect of studies of refugee children in school made it clear that 'PTSD [post-traumatic stress disorder] symptoms, affective symptoms or language difficulties were manifesting in the classrooms as inattention, fidgeting and distractibility' (O'Shea *et al.*, 2000, p. 193). It is clear that the tutor's sympathetic observation is important for diagnosis, and that his or her calm, firm, start-of-the-day reminders and end-of-the-day enquiries are especially needed and valuable.

It is truly difficult for most of us fully to understand the experiences, fears and sadnesses of a pupil's parents or carers, but the tutor should do all he or she can, including some background research reading of the particular family's previous country. It is also extremely helpful to talk about such experiences with others who have had first-hand experience. We strongly recommend the tutor makes special efforts to keep in touch with these parents: the personal voice of contact is especially supportive.

## Getting to know the tutee

In essence, the first steps are the same as those outlined for families (see page 97). The pupil's file is not a sufficient tool on its own but is a necessary start too often overlooked. The shrewd tutor looks for the euphemistic phrase from the primary school, the tell-tale worried remark, along with the achievements, interests and characteristics. Of course, there are dangers in being too influenced by the past. Every pupil must be allowed to have a new future. On the other hand, a child is not a *tabula rasa*, and to seek to erase the growth of primary school years is naive and counter-productive.

'The child is father of the man' and the continuities of growth are as strong as the discontinuities (see Robins and Rutter, 1990). No tutor would wish to judge a pupil's present or future potential from the records of the past. On the other hand, it would be rash not to make careful use of the records. It is amateur to say: 'I don't like to know too much about a pupil's past.' The professional need is to know and the professional skill is to make good use of the information available. The vital first step is a sensitive study of records, tempered by a refusal to 'label'.

This is equally true for the pupil being taken over in mid-stream by a tutor after a year or more in the secondary school. In this case, the immediacy of the records and the fact that the notes, reports or letters in the file have been written by the tutor's colleagues makes fresh judgement more difficult. The new tutor must make as conscious an effort to read and listen when he takes a group over as when the pupils are new to the school. Following discussions with the previous tutor and careful study of the files, the tutor newly taking a group will want to schedule a series of personal meetings along the lines we described.

## Looking forward

There is, though, another weakness to do with the past – one which is perhaps an even deeper problem. Most tutor–pupil meetings are *retrospective* – as are most personal guidance sessions in secondary schools. We do our best to help a pupil cope with her problems *after* some difficulty, upsetting event, failure or missed opportunity. The ratio in our tutoring of time spent mopping up to time spent enabling pupils to avoid trouble and to make good use of opportunities is sadly unbalanced. Pupils face so many of the choices and challenges of their schooling unprepared. Too often they are taken by surprise.

A planned tutorial programme and whole-group tutoring are the broad, fundamental bases of pastoral care – and make the major contribution to shifting pastoral care from reactive to proactive. Individual work too has to have this proactive component: to talk after the event is not making the best use of talking.

Routine review meetings have the advantage of not having to deal with a recent 'problem' or being permeated by the tension of teacher reprimanding pupil. Their disadvantage is that, lacking immediate purpose, they may seem pointless. The tutor should therefore consider the following approaches.

1. Relate scheduled review meetings to the tutorial programme, so that pupils not only know that they are coming and do not associate them (as they do most meetings with teachers) with 'trouble', but also understand their purpose.
2. Make the main format of the meetings clear in advance and especially what it would be helpful for pupils to think over beforehand.
3. Structure the meeting so that the pupil can raise matters and has space to respond personally, and also so that the talk is not merely desultory – the pupil should be conscious that major aspects of her developing 'pupilship' are being covered.
4. Whenever appropriate, relate the individual discussion to aspects of the group-work and the tutorial programme.

There is an educative reciprocity when tutorial-programme issues feed in as background and, conversely, when the depth of individual tutor–pupil discussion can be used by the pupil in group work.

Finally, such meetings ought ideally to end with a summary: 'So we are agreed that . . .'. And the pupil should feel some ownership of this summary, being free to add: 'But please don't forget that I . . .' or to contradict: 'Is that fair when you agreed that I did . . . ?' In years ten and eleven, this will be part of the Progress File, but the *process* should be regularly revisited from about the end of the first term – and from, say, year nine the tutor could give the pupil a written copy of such a summary.

## Monitoring

The tutor will receive from around the school a plethora of signals of varying degrees of authenticity about his tutees. Some will be contradictory, and most will be critical, however good the pupil. It is a sad fact that we find the time and energy to pass on encouraging news less often.

A tutor needs to extend and complement this unsolicited selection of comments by specific enquiries, both as routine (for example, as part of school reports home) or when occasion arises (such as when considering the overall situation of a pupil before meeting her parents). Some schools have standard comment sheets to circulate; some tutors prefer to send their colleagues a simple note:

*This copy for . . . . . . . .*

*Memorandum to all teachers of Leroy Foot*

*Because of his family's worries about whether he is under-achieving and whether we are setting him stretching enough assignments, I am reviewing Leroy's work and attainment and meeting his parents on Tuesday after half term.*

*Could you please return this slip to me with your estimate of his achievement in this first half term of the course. I would especially appreciate any views on whether he finds the work too easy and how much effort he appears to be putting into the work you set.*

*Could you please return this by October 15ᵗʰ. Thank you very much!*

*Re: Leroy Foot*

*Memorandum to Mohammed Kassim, Tutor of Leroy Foot*

*Subject:* . . . . . . . . . . .     *Teacher's Name* . . . . . . . . . . . .

*Signed* . . . . . . . . . . . .
*Date* . . . . . . . . . . . . . . . . . . . . . .

The cumulative sequence of work in ordinary exercise books and folders is, of course, the main signalling a tutor receives. No tutor could review all this work regularly, but from time to time it is well worth looking at a sample of each pupil's work. You do not have to be a subject expert to get an impression – and only the tutor is in a position of having an overview of *all* the work.

## The time and the place

Every tutor, therefore, needs to allow time for:

- a rota of review sessions
- booked sessions for unplanned but not necessarily 'emergency' talks

But where? Although two people can have valuable exchanges on the run as they move from one place to another, for the tutor to have one of the key tutoring tasks scheduled for the corridor is just careless.

Of course, many significant exchanges inevitably and properly arise out of whole-group sessions or recent experiences, gaining in immediacy what they lose in tranquillity from a brief on-the-spot word: 'You seemed upset then, Omar.' 'Did you really mean to be so cutting, Janice?' 'Leroy, I thought you were really helpful to Mary.'

The tutor has to respond to the pupil rushing in at the end of the afternoon with a tale of woe from her English lesson, to the news picked up during the day that a boy's sister has died, or to a girl being accused of stealing a purse. Such moments will occur by the door, in the corridor, in the corner of the room, or sometimes, thankfully, with the tutor seated by her desk and the pupil beside her, despite the activities of others in the room.

The unplanned will demand this awkwardness of time and place but this is not good enough for all aspects of consistent individual tutoring. At least, the tutor will want to see some of the pupils when the tide of the day has ebbed and he can sit with the pupil in an almost quiet room. However, the full tutor room is not best suited for such counselling sessions and every tutor should, if possible, have the use of a study or office.

Had pastoral care been properly defined in the 1950s and its equipment and architectural requirement properly articulated, interview rooms would no doubt have been as much a part of the standard spaces of schools as laboratories and libraries. As it is, pastoral care team leaders are still often without private rooms.

There are, though, advantages in using the tutor's and tutor group's own classroom. Creating a 'tutor room' out of a classroom can make pupils feel it is their 'home room' (that pleasant American high school phrase), and help the tutor create an excellent ambience for a meeting.

Nevertheless, tutors should seek access to suitable interview and discussion rooms, which are there for booking in meetings with parents, carers, specialist support staff, or the pupils themselves. Complementary or alternative arrangements can be made to use the temporarily vacant offices of head or deputies. While sometimes awkward, this option should not be dismissed.

As a workable routine, the tutor should have one scheduled interview with each of her tutees in a quiet, private and comfortable room once a term, with further opportunities for similar interviews as required.

## Recording

A frequent fault when helping pupils is to overemphasize our individual contribution and to see a particular meeting as separate from the longer-term approach. This leads to being less meticulous about recording.

A pupil's file should be seen as a diagnostic tool of pastoral care, helping reflection, analysis and plans for action. The pupil should know of its existence and of its uses. She should sometimes be asked to suggest anything about the term's work and events that ought to go in it. The tutor should ensure that notes on major and minor points are included and, however brief, dated.

We have suggested regular review interviews for pupils, and the tutor should also have interviews with families, the number of which will depend on the way the pastoral aspect of the school is devolved. For example, some schools have reception or option interviews carried out by middle or senior management responsible for pastoral care; others give some of this work to tutors – a practice we prefer.

It is essential that a record of every interview is kept to retain continuity, progress and parents' confidence. Unless the teacher is able to write up the interview immediately it ends, he should take short notes during the interview – discreetly but not secretly. It is as well to say that one is noting the things agreed and the action to be taken by the school. Indeed, failure to do so undermines parents' confidence and such failures are often referred to in later interviews.

Writing up the interview must be done as soon as possible as, even with outline notes, it is easy to forget what was said and decided. At the end of the interview, give a summary of any decisions or recommendations made. In some cases, a letter should follow setting them out clearly. Also keep colleagues informed, especially with a note of any action promised.

A meticulous and coherent process of recording can be invaluable well beyond the immediate support it provides for the tutor's own responsibilities. For example, with special educational needs although the Special Educational Needs Coordinator (SENCO) will be the formal contact with a pupil's family and with outside agencies, the tutor must also be sufficiently in touch with a pupil's life to be able to play a key role in the information-gathering, consultative and assessment tasks set out in the *Code of Practice* on the identification and assessment of special educational needs (DfES, 2001a). Similarly, such a process can inform the teacher designated to advocate for children and young people in public care and help in developing a pupil's Personal Education Plan (DH/DfES, 2000).

## The hierarchical team

Schools sometimes find the vertical hierarchy of team leadership difficult to accept, still more to use effectively. Too easily, mistrust develops, part of the institutional culture of a secondary school, in which the greatest time and emphasis is properly given to classroom teaching and the relationship of teacher to taught is the one understood best. The result can be that a school is less clear about the referral of an individual or particular group. Indeed, disruptive behaviour is sometimes regarded as the only trigger for complaint, and methodical consultation and referral are less common.

Ideally, the tutor should routinely review the progress of all aspects of her tutees with the team leader, say every half term. These occasions allow for reflection on each pupil prompted by the senior colleague that is different from the daily rush. The less demanding tutee can be focused on: 'What does she need?' 'How is he developing?'

Pupils causing concern can be reviewed in terms of action planned: 'Has the daily report helped her?' 'Is his family making the promised weekly contact?' This is the time for plans to be changed to ensure a coherent and continuously applied regime for the more worrying pupils. (Of course, the middle management pastoral team leader needs similar reviews, concentrating on the more difficult cases, with the appropriate member of the senior management team.) Such opportunities can convert individual casework from reactive to proactive, and give the daily challenges of the weeks ahead a positive and hopeful coherence. They can also ensure that no one is overlooked because she or he is 'getting along OK'.

Whether or not you have such review sessions in your team, you need to consult over individual pupils. The criterion for this is not the seriousness of the situation, but the need for a second opinion. A major family bereavement or an unpleasant incident of racial harassment may be more serious than the boy who is just jogging along, but the action required on the first two may be obvious and that on the third baffling. A tutor always needs to keep the team leader informed, but it is much harder to know when a second opinion is valuable.

It can be hard to know who is taking responsibility in such cases of collaboration.

Are you:

1. Merely informing? e.g. Tom's father has come back from abroad.
2. Informing and suggesting simple action supportive to you? e.g. Happy Begum's father has died after a long illness; would you please send a letter on behalf of the school?
3. Consulting? e.g. Martin is being kept away from school and my notes are getting nowhere; any ideas?
4. Referring? e.g. I've done all I can to help Leila get herself to school on time; could you please take over?

Clarity of responsibility is essential. In cases of referral, it is wise to be sure which aspects are being referred, and to have a clear return handback. You cannot afford to be confused about who is currently responsible for particular aspects of care.

The good tutor is not one who manages to handle everything herself, but one who knows how to use her team leader and other specialists, including support staff, consulting, seeking help and referring sensitively.

# 8 Working with others

## Introduction

Teaching tends to be thought of fairly often as working as an individual. Our professional traditions have not included much emphasis on working with others, especially those we used to call 'non-teachers'. Indeed there were many schools which were what we call 'professio-centric', that is attitudinally denigrating those who do not teach, including, for example, social workers. In recent years there has been a huge improvement in teamwork within the teaching staff of schools, and between teaching and the expanding range of support staff, including teaching assistants. Similarly, a school's teachers are usually working more closely with the range of supportive specialists such as attendance officers, behaviour improvement assistants, Connexions personal advisers, and family workers.

Those working with children and families are therefore more numerous and have more responsibilities. This affects all the staff of a school, but especially enriches the work of form tutors – as well as adding to the extent of their administration and communication work. The more fully you work *with* this range of staff the more effective your tutoring will be, and the greater the potential personal and study growth of your own tutees. In this section we give some examples.

## External support

Just as the pastoral staff inside a school have to work as a team, so the school has to collaborate with the range of other children-related agencies outside the school. Proposed reforms to children's services, first set out in the DfES Green Paper *Every Child Matters* in September 2003, consolidate and extend the increasing coordination and interaction between children's services and the education, health, legal and vocational services.

In many respects, this approach is underscoring what is already seen as a key role by the form tutor. Certainly, one of the tutor's skills is to ensure pupils and their families are in touch with appropriate specialist agencies, and to work with those same agencies in the interests of the pupil. Indeed, in the first decade of this century one of the key movements in schooling has been the development of a range of school support staff and specialist workers.

Each school will already have its own arrangements for collaborating with such agencies. The tutor, however, will be expected in most cases to be the first point of contact and diagnosis of possible need – and thereby remains a key figure. What, though, should the tutor be looking for?

First, a school will want its pupils to have the minimum physical and financial necessities. The tutor will therefore be alert to any signs of acute poverty, inadequate clothing, news of housing difficulties, clues of heating deficiencies. Any worries should be treated sensitively, followed up and suitable help sought through the Education Welfare Service or Social Services Department. Such problems will need to be referred to the middle management pastoral care team leader, and sometimes to the specialist external support worker. But the tutor is best placed to pick up the clues and start the ball rolling.

Second, the tutor will watch out for apparent health problems. Of course, almost every pupil comes into secondary school with a medical record and routine medicals follow. Although legislation does not require a school health service, the Department of Health sees 'a continuing and evolving role' for such a service with teachers playing an 'essential' part in it (Department of Health, 1996). The British Paediatric Association has argued that 'a school-based service provides a unique opportunity for assessing children and young people in a child-centred, educational environment' (BPA, 1995).

The lay eye of the tutor is a necessary component: are there any unexpected signs about complexion, breathing, eyes, hearing, movements? Hearing difficulties can go undiagnosed because they are intermittent, but they can substantially impede learning. The tutor can pick up on comments by subject teachers, be observant, suitably enquiring and ready to discuss and refer. Although families are understandably sensitive to suggestions that there is undiagnosed ill health, the tutor is the best-placed professional to notice when it does occur.

The introduction of personal, social and health education (PSHE) and citizenship has been accompanied by greater support for schools in these areas, through, for example, healthy schools partnerships under the National Healthy School Standard. This is encouraging a 'whole school approach' to PSHE that covers leadership, policy development, curriculum planning and resourcing, teaching and learning, school culture and environment, giving pupils a voice, the provision of pupils' support services, staff professional development, partnership with parents and local communities, and assessing, recording and reporting pupils' achievement. This should lead to a growing school-wide awareness of health issues and underpin the tutor's role here.

## Child protection

The form tutor must also be prepared to handle extreme situations, such as child abuse – emotional, physical or specifically sexual. Such abuse has been increasingly recognized as awareness of its frequency has grown. There is, however, no easy formula for recognizing sexual abuse, and the evidence is that many young people still keep their secret uncomfortably but successfully to themselves. Nevertheless, there will be times when the tutor picks up hints or is even taken into a pupil's confidence, however tentatively and indirectly.

Much sexual abuse is not revealed in any ostensible signs. Nevertheless, the tutor sensitive and alert to any aspects of behaviour, remarks or physical indications is more likely than anyone else to notice key clues. These can range from tense, vulnerable, closing-in behaviour to undue sexual awareness with younger children – indeed, in some cases an abused pupil may be an abuser too.

The tutor who has established a close, mutually respectful relationship is more likely to receive spoken hints or outright pleas for help. However, tutors must not feel guilty if abuse is found but nothing has been volunteered. It is very difficult for the abused to talk.

Care has to be taken over promises of confidentiality: a tutor cannot give a blanket promise, and should make clear that dangerous and illegal activities may well have to be passed on – for the pupil's own welfare.

This is another example of how individual casework should relate to the overall tutorial programme. A well-prepared part of the programme allows the abused young person to bring into his consciousness that abusive behaviour which very likely has been suppressed. It also allows the pupil to formulate concepts and to develop language which help him to 'objectivise' the experience – and this makes it easier for the pupil to talk about it. Opposite is an example of a year-eight worksheet which puts the most frequent assumptions about child sexual abuse against the surveyed facts. This is one of the aspects of pastoral care which causes tutors most distress. It is emotionally and mentally painful for us to think about; it is doubly distressing to consider one of our pupils having experienced such abuse; we worry about our comparative ignorance; we fret about the legal situations – and we know of the huge public controversies that have raged.

The particular tension at the heart of the tutorial role is the fact that most sexual abuse is within the family circle; the victim is torn between affection and love for the abuser and abhorrence – often feeling an unreasonable guilt herself, and dreading the consequences of revelation.

Clearly, the tutor should not hang on to his doubts or suspicions for very long: this is a key instance of the importance of teamwork. The tutor's task is not to be an expert in child sexual abuse – nor to investigate suspected abuse herself – but to be an expert on her pupils, noticing signs of fear, sexual provocativeness, being withdrawn, flinching or just plain misery.

The tutor will hope that the background overall tutorial programme and the mutual trust of tutor and pupil will permit talk. But the tutor must not be disappointed or resentful if the abused pupil cannot share the distress.

Every school should now have specific procedures, of which all staff should be aware, for handling suspected cases of abuse, designating a senior member of staff to coordinate action within

## Getting to know yourself

What is the sexual assault of a child?

Sexual assault means forcing somebody to be involved in sexual contact. When you're older, sexual contact will make you feel close, happy, excited, loving and reassured. Much of your happiness will come from choosing to be close to the other person, and it will involve feeling that all of your body and your thoughts and feelings are valued. Sexual assault is different because you are not choosing and how you feel comes second to the other person's feelings. When children are victims of sexual assault, the sexual contact may involve handling of the child's genitals or the child may be asked to touch the genitals of the older child or adult. Sometimes the contact can be oral sex, using the child's mouth. Sexual contact can include trying to be inside the vagina or anus. Other kinds of assault don't involve any physical contact; a child may be forced to look at the genitals of another person or to undress. Whatever happens, children can't be ready for sexual contact with another person until they have grown up, and can choose for themselves what they want to do.

What most people think happens when a child is assaulted and what really happens are often quite different.

| What most people think | What is much more common |
| --- | --- |
| A dangerous, weird stranger | A person they know, often a relative or friend of the family, is more often the case (85 per cent of cases) |
| Isolated incident | Over and over again |
| Out of the blue | A situation that develops gradually over a period of time |
| Rare and extreme | Frequent incidents. There are many forms of sexual assault |
| A violent attack | Subtle, rather than extreme force |

the school and liaise with outside agencies (DfEE Circular 10/95 *Protecting Children from Abuse: the Role of the Education Service*, 1995a).

The earliest worries should be discussed with the pastoral team leader. It is usually unwise to share initial concerns with other colleagues. This is possibly the most highly charged aspect of pastoral care. The pastoral team leader will normally discuss the matter with – depending on local arrangements – the education welfare officer, the LEA's child protection coordinator, the local social services department, a member of the school support staff, or the NSPCC. Whoever is consulted, the tutor should always remain part of the team. Wise pastoral care procedures in schools keep the tutor as an active part of the team throughout: he has the widest knowledge of the young person, the daily contact and the continuing responsibility.

The Children Act 1989 prompted greater inter-agency cooperation on matters such as child protection and family support, under the general term of *Working Together*. This has developed extensively in the subsequent years. Area Child Protection Committees (ACPCs) provide a forum for the various professions jointly to develop, monitor and review local child protection policies and promote effective cooperation between the agencies involved, including schools. Such collaboration would also go on in individual child protection conferences to which the Tutor may well be asked to contribute a written report on a child suspected of being abused, or even to participate.

## Effective collaboration

As we have said, teachers are not at their best working with professionals outside teaching on whatever issue, for we usually have no training and little experience. For example, we tend to underestimate the work of education welfare officers, sometimes treating them merely as messengers to take the school's wishes to elusive families. More generally, we tend to distrust the 'lack of understanding' of psychologist, social worker, counsellor, or physician, who does not work in schools. But rather than setting out straightaway to persuade them to our point of view, we should relish theirs. The education welfare officer, for example, rightly has a different point of view, speaking for the overall needs of a pupil as a person and not primarily for the overall needs of the class. Disagreements with other professionals are inevitable and not unhealthy. Indeed, it is dangerous to presume that we all have or should have the same perspective. It is professional to disagree.

The General Teaching Council for England (GTCE) emphasizes that, quite rightly, schools have developed a range of different structures to manage other adults involved in teaching and learning:

> There will be no single model because school arrangements will need to make sense in the context of the tasks assigned to different staff. However, it is important that expectations about the number and range of other adults a teacher might work with at any given time are reasonable.
>
> (GTCE, 2002)

The arrangements made should encompass external support specialists as well.

A review of studies and evaluations of multi-agency initiatives has identified some of the key factors in successful partnerships between professionals from different education, social and health agencies (Tomlinson, 2003). These include:

- strategic and operational commitment to collaboration
- awareness of agencies' differing aims and values, with a commitment to working towards a common goal
- involvement of all relevant people, often including clients and their carers
- clear roles and responsibilities for individuals and agencies involved in collaboration
- supportive and committed management of staff in partnerships
- flexible and innovative funding mechanisms
- systems for inter-agency collecting, sharing and analysis of data
- joint training, with accreditation where appropriate
- strategies to encourage team commitment beyond the personal interests of key individuals

- effective and appropriate communication between agencies and professionals
- a suitable, and sometimes altered, location for the delivery of services

One example drawn on is Durham County Council's joint Education and Child and Adolescent Mental Health Services (CAMHS) consultation forum on children reluctant to attend school. The forum meetings enabled the different professionals to consider together the referred case, reach a common understanding of the problems, and agree a realistic plan specifying targets and agencies to be involved. The schools used the meetings to obtain advice from the various agencies, and to plan and monitor a pupil's progress.

## Attendance

Managing attendance in schools is now a substantial and sophisticated process that involves wide-ranging government policies backed by legislation, new sets of advisers and support teams, and a growth in local and internet sources of advice for teachers. This both reflects and drives the greater integration of issues of attendance and truancy into the overall personal development of all pupils, and a school's whole teaching and learning curriculum. In short, every staff member in a school now has an increased responsibility for, and stake in, matters of 'attendance'.

The Anti-social Behaviour Act 2003 introduces a balanced, if rigorous, legal framework of support and sanctions around school attendance and behaviour that embraces LEAs, schools, and parents or carers. Registration in schools is increasingly being carried out through electronic registration systems, which are more reliable, speedy and accessible to more staff within and beyond the school. An attendance officer in each school now takes on the daily task of following up on non-attendance. Education welfare officers (EWOs) are being devolved to schools, and the service is establishing new national occupational standards. Multi-agency Behaviour and Education Support Teams (BESTs) are being set up in LEAs to provide support in schools and the community for identifying, intervening in and managing emotional and behaviour issues in children. These teams form part of wider Behaviour Improvement Programmes in some areas.

All these elements are underpinned by the government's Behaviour and Attendance Strategy providing more resources and advice to LEAs, schools and teachers in improving pupils' attendance and behaviour.

## The tutor's role in the behaviour and attendance strategy

These developments inevitably have an impact on the tutor's role and organization within the school. There are risks of that role losing clarity and thereby the tutor becomes, or feels, marginalized or disempowered, especially as guidance on the new policies and schemes do not always make explicit reference to the tutor's role within them.

For example, the use of an attendance officer to follow up absences through first-day calling has relieved the tutor of a time-consuming task – as well as providing an immediate and consistent response. However, this only works properly if the tutor is able to share the information and insights of the attendance officers.

The vital dialogue between tutor and tutee – and the tutee's home – must remain at the core of all these changes. Schools should therefore continue to make explicit, both in terms of organization and policy, that the tutor retains the key role in probing and understanding reasons for absence, and its consequences, and in offering the appropriate care for the tutee. The tutor, of course, must have ready access to all the information about a tutee in whatever form such material is collected and held.

The tutor's centrality should also be extended to leading on schemes to promote and celebrate positive attendance, such as 100 per cent attendance clubs, rolls of honour, and good attendance stickers and certificates, and to the school's behaviour and attendance curriculum programme.

The challenge, then, is to embrace the benefits of these new strategies and systems and, at the same time, to incorporate them into the school's, and more specifically, the tutor's own effective ways of working with tutees.

It is up to each school to determine how best to establish and adapt the current initiatives, such as electronic registration system (e-registration), behaviour and education support team (BEST), a devolved education welfare officer, so that they are compatible with the school's own pastoral ethos and good practice.

A first step might be to re-visit the tutor's job description in order to clarify the responsibilities and opportunities being established by the new legislative and advisory frameworks.

### The tutor and the behaviour and attendance curriculum

The tutor is crucial in guiding or managing the school's behaviour and attendance curriculum. For example, the behaviour and attendance strand of the Key Stage 3 strategy makes it clear that the school's responsibility extends beyond managing behaviour to teaching those positive behaviours that promote effective learning. Subject departments are responsible for teaching tutees what each particular subject demands in terms of behaviour. But the tutor can coordinate these activities by teaching cross-subject learning behaviours and engaging tutees in appreciating the value of attendance and punctuality.

### The tutor and behaviour management systems

Positive behaviour systems, such as assertive discipline, can promote a consistent response to tutees' choices. The risk is that they encourage an 'automatic' response, such as so many warnings triggers a given tariff of responses. The tutor can prevent this by being in an acknowledged position to analyse patterns of incident, identify problem relationships or subject areas, and flag up potential learning needs. This enables the tutor to broker a reconciliation between tutee and staff member, or to monitor and advertise successful and not so successful efforts at improvement.

The point is that unless the tutor has the space and the information within which to do this, it will appear, mistakenly, that behaviour management systems can run on their own. The system can impede, rather than enhance, the tutor's role. Technological intelligence can overwhelm emotional intelligence.

### The tutor and the key worker

The 'key worker' is becoming an increasingly familiar member of a school's professional network, particular those involved in the Behaviour Improvement Programme (BIP) in Excellence in Cities areas. A key worker can be allocated to a child who has been identified as at risk or having specific needs in order to coordinate support or liaise between various relevant agencies. Sometimes, the tutor can be given this role. Where not, the details of the relationship between key worker and tutor should be discussed and agreed, especially over the sharing of information. This can avoid cutting the tutor out of the BIP process – or indeed any scheme where other professionals take a leading, and tutor-related, role in supporting a tutee.

### The tutor and individual plans

When a tutee is given an individual support plan, such as a pastoral support plan (PSP), individual education plan (IEP), or individual behaviour plan (IBP), the tutor should play the main part in drawing it up, running it, and monitoring its effectiveness. Some schools fail to make the tutor's role in such plans explicit enough.

## Year or House team leader

Every form tutor needs to work closely with her or his team leader, usually titled 'year head', but sometimes a 'head of house'. This is a more difficult professional relationship than with your head of subject department (HoD), for a number of reasons:

- the HoD usually took part in your selection and appointment, knows you from the interview, and was mostly responsible for your induction
- most subject departments have regular meetings and all have a promulgated scheme of work for their curriculum. Thus as a subject teachers you have a continuous working relationship with your HoD and her or his deputies
- you normally stay in that department team continuously and thus work with the same leader over many years

Year heads often do not know who their tutors will be until late in the planning for the next year. They sometimes then have tutors with whom they have not worked before and they see far less of their year tutors' pastoral work than your subject HoD does of your subject teaching.

Further, the year head's non-teaching time is extremely tightly filled with family and pupil casework and reviewing external agencies, and she or he frequently has even less time for team leadership than a head of department. In some schools the year head role is perceived as being responsible for pupils rather than including the leadership of tutors.

Therefore, use every way you can to get to know your year head, such as asking his or her advice, requesting to read pupils' files, giving views about the individual pupils, and taking a supportive part in tutor meetings. It is most important to consult on the inevitably many matters about care of pupils and families on which even an experienced tutor benefits from a second opinion.

## Relating to subject-teaching colleagues

One of the hardest aspects of tutoring is relating to the needs of the pupils on the one hand and to the responses of colleagues on the other. A tutor is likely to find a number of occasions when his personal and professional loyalty is strained by allegations from a pupil that a teaching colleague is treating him wrongly or unfairly. 'Miss, that Mr Charles, do you know what he called me?' 'Sir, it doesn't matter what I do in Jones', I mean Mr Jones' class, he always picks on me, just for breathing funny like, the moment I come in the room!'

The traditional camaraderie of the staff has an unspoken principle that an offence against one is an offence against all – and, even more dubiously, that the judge of whether a look, word or act is an offence is the teacher who has been offended. Some schools have established whole-school disciplinary codes to avoid the grosser offences. This is required under current conditions of service and by Section 22 of the Education (No 2) Act 1986. Even with such statements, though, there will be variations between colleagues and allegations will continue to fly between pupil and teacher.

No advice can meet all occasions. But some principles can be established. First, don't react too quickly or jump to a conclusion at the initial description of what 'happened': things are rarely as they seem, especially when pupil and teacher worlds collide. Pupils have to learn that ill-considered complaints will not be taken at face value and that criticisms of teachers cannot be offered as a mere defence in a pre-emptive strike. On the other hand, they must also trust that their tutor will listen and support them when appropriate. A tutor's professional integrity is thus tested.

There will be times when you will need to help your tutee towards a reconciliation when he has been in the wrong. This is the educational heart of tutoring because it enables the tutee to reflect, understand how and why he went wrong, and to devise suitable ways to apologize and make positive moves forward – wiser, chastened perhaps, but not humiliated.

When, though, it is patently clear that the other teacher is wrong, the problem is greater. You are responsible for your tutee's behaviour but not for your colleague's. If your tutee is merely misunderstood, a chat with your colleague may allow her to see the pupil in a different light. If there has been a factual misunderstanding, it is not too difficult to put right. However, there might be occasions when your tutee has suffered a definite indignity from unprofessional conduct: a physical punishment, a racist remark, a family jibe. The pupil has the right to look to you for support.

It is at such times that your reputation for evenhandedness will be scrutinized. You may be able to have a friendly, even jocular word, with the colleague concerned. If she concedes, the problem can be readily resolved, and you can attempt a reconciliation by taking your tutee to see the colleague. If, however, there is no offer or concession, you have a stark choice between staffroom comfort and professional comfort, but you cannot choose to ignore the situation.

If the event is not too serious or hurtful, you can counsel the pupil to let it pass on the grounds that some unpleasantnesses and even injustices are not worth fighting and are best forgiven or forgotten – and in doing so coming out the 'bigger' person, winning by not fighting. On the other hand, you may have to face your colleague with the awkward position that you are in: you cannot silently overlook the fact that he hit your tutee or she used racist language. If the incident was an inadvertent, momentary slip, surely we can find a way to reconciliation. However, if that is not acceptable to your colleague, you are sorry but you simply have to ask someone to take it over.

Such action is the professional thing to do: your duty as a tutor is to ensure your tutees have their entitlement at school, and that includes fairness, protection from violence, and protection from improper personal remarks.

In some ways, an even trickier problem is the more intangible complaint, such as: 'She doesn't do anything with me, Sir!' 'He can't keep us in order, really.' As the tutor's task is to assist her tutees towards their entitlement, she must be distressed at the suggestion that they are having unsatisfactory subject teaching in whatever way. The tutorial period discussion has to be handled with care:

- can the tutees express their disquiet courteously and without rancour?
- can they be precise without exaggeration?
- can they consider what in their behaviour individually or severally may have contributed to or even created the difficulty?
- can the tutor group as a whole find a way of putting its view to that teacher?

It will be seen that, as in so much of tutoring, reacting to events and caring for the individual have a reciprocal relationship with whole-group, underlying tutorial work. Such discussions should be underpinned by the tutorial programme approach to getting on and not getting on with people (see Chapter 4, pages 67–78). The particular discussion of *this* sequence of events will itself be part of the 'programme', real and immediate 'material' to join the simulated, factual or fictional material of the presented programme. 'What,' asks the tutor, 'can we do?' If the group admits some culpability, the group can find ways to put that right and apologize. If not, the task of responsibility for the action must lie with the tutor. The tutees have played their role by sharing their grievance with their tutor. If the tutor cannot decently see it as a mere temporary aberration and help the individual or group to accept it, she must take the matter up in confidence with the individual, her team leader, or the tutor's team leader.

# Mentors

Mentoring is a term often used quite loosely to describe a range of activities. All involve a one-to-one relationship in which the mentor aims to help the mentee develop personally. Traditionally, mentoring involves a volunteer from the business world or local community who endeavours to support a young person's development socially and emotionally. Other common schemes are peer mentoring and learning mentoring. The former involves an older student as mentor who befriends and supports a younger pupil. The latter focuses particularly on helping young people organize their workload in school in order to improve achievement.

All mentoring stresses the importance of building a positive relationship as the basis for change. A mentor aims to work in partnership with a young person to help him or her feel valued, to be able to communicate more effectively, develop relationships and to be better prepared for adult life. Any gains in self-confidence facilitate improvements in self-development and achievement.

The National Mentoring Network's *Advice for Mentors Working in Schools* (2002) states that: 'As a mentor, you will be providing a less experienced individual with the benefit of your life, school or work experience with a view to encouraging the student to move confidently through a range of new experiences – in short, someone to learn from.'

In many ways the mentor relates to a mentee similarly to how a form tutor does:

- get to know the student and build together
- establish the general objectives that they will aim to work towards together
- encourage students to do their best
- listen to what they say, value their opinions and beliefs, and treat as a priority anything that is worrying them
- encourage them to talk about their hopes and ambitions
- talk about relevant experiences they have had and, as appropriate, about problems they have overcome
- talk about the world of work and the expectations of employers

- take an interest in the students, their study and their lives
- set realistic and manageable targets together, e.g. homework deadlines, and other time management goals
- celebrate the students' efforts and successes

They may also:

- ask for a tour of the school
- arrange a visit to their own place of work
- discuss work experience or interview techniques
- visit a lesson or form tutor period
- give practical help with project work where they have appropriate skills

Many students come to regard their mentor as a 'friend'. As an adult, the mentor has 'befriended' the young person while maintaining the boundaries appropriate for an informal professional relationship. The tutor therefore needs to find out if there is an established mentoring scheme and, if so, who does the mentoring. Does the school have a mentoring coordinator? If so, find out her or his job description and make contact.

From within the school, find out: Is there peer monitoring? Does the senior management team (SMT) mentor any students, for example, Year 11 pupils? Do any other teachers or teaching assistants mentor pupils? And from outside the school, find out: What organizations carry out mentoring in the school?

The process of mentoring is valuable not only to young people with specific difficulties. Indeed, we all benefit from a quasimentor. Many adults when they look back on the crucially positive development in their life recognize that a particular adult who was not a parent or a teacher listened to them, shared ideas with them, and encouraged them in private, individual meetings. Some schools have a wide, all-embracing scheme. For instance, Michael Marland as a headteacher in a London comprehensive arranged mentoring for all possible university applicants and for all Year 10 pupils. Some schools have a general availability without definition and tutors can recommend for a variety of reasons, including further encouragement for happy and successful pupils. For instance, a pupil with a keen interest in a particular topic, an art, sport or an occupation will often really benefit from a mentor to share that enthusiasm. Often, an able and keen student without a particular focus of ambition develops a wide range of interests in this way. Pupils of many ethnic backgrounds find a mentor of that ethnicity especially encouraging, particularly if they are locally in a minority.

Disaffected students or those with specific difficulties will almost certainly benefit from having a mentor. Indicators of disaffection and difficulties include:

- a drop in tests/exams/continuous assessment over time (not just a one off)
- tests/exams/continuous assessment results have been in the lowest quartile of the class over a period of time
- a pupil has been absent from school due to truanting, exclusion or sickness more than average
- a pupil has a reading age below that expected for his or her age (has he or she also been assessed for Specific Learning Difficulties?)
- a pupil lives in an area that has particular social problems
- a pupil has been cautioned by the police, convicted of a crime or re-offended
- a pupil does not seem to have a supportive family environment (e.g. his or her parents may not turn up for parents' evenings, she or he may not be dressed smartly or may not have a quiet place in which to do homework)
- a pupil appears to interact poorly with peers or adults
- a pupil appears to exhibit a low level of self-confidence or self-esteem (e.g. he or she may be very quiet or too boisterous, involved in bullying, etc.)

(Adapted from the Kent Start Project)

Some students may not wish the fact that they have a mentor to be referred to publicly and their wishes should be respected. If the student agrees, however, it may be possible to meet the mentor or at least contact them so that the lines of communication are clear if you should wish to pass on any concerns or information about a student's successes.

## Conclusion

However caring, ambitious, and hardworking, a tutor is not ultimately responsible for all aspects of his tutees and must not feel overburdened: the hierarchical structure must be able to take over. The school's responsibility for the welfare and growth of the individual pupil is lodged with the tutor 'in the first instance'. The tutor's art and craft has two aspects: the first is to relate individual casework to whole-group discussion and the tutorial programme; the second is to know when to hand over to his or her senior. A form tutor cannot keep a tutee to him- or herself: the school's teamwork is required.

# 9 The Form Tutor's style

## Introduction

Perhaps more than in any other aspect of teaching, the successful Form Tutor is one who uses but does not exploit her or his own personality and personal approaches. In all roles in a school there is a tension between self and task, which can be fruitful or destructive.

There is clearly a problem of confidentiality: one of the main reasons for locating such a major curriculum responsibility in the tutorial programme under the Heads of Year is to link the personal and social development aspects of the whole-school curriculum with the very close knowledge of the pupil and his or her family that Year Head and tutor have. For instance, a tutor will have read all the files of her tutees; a subject teacher cannot do all this for every pupil in all her classes, or indeed for any but a handful. This knowledge which the tutor has makes links between pupil situations and the topic and the learning material possible and profitable, but it also risks revealing confidential knowledge. The tutor will have to guard against this, while not wishing to lose or waste the intimacy of his or her knowledge.

## The tutorial environment

Ideally, a whole school community should be characterized by quiet, good organization that encourages all the teachers to relate warmly though clearly and firmly to all students. Schools where a combination of architectural, organizational, student composition, and staffing problems lead to tensions and confrontations will be communities in which it is considerably harder for any teacher to work effectively for the students' personal and social development. Some schools offer an unsympathetic environment. Many, indeed, are harsh physical environments in which wall textures, acoustics, graffiti and the ugly combine to create a need to shout, be surly and be tense. A few are visually starved of works of art, pupils' work, interesting displays, signs of the real world or, indeed, anything on which the eye can light with pleasure.

In such schools and in others better placed physically there can be an inter-personal regime that is equally destructive: adults ignore pupils, are abrupt, shout or are sarcastic. The procedures lack warmth and dignity.

Instead, the school as a whole should be a warm, celebratory, flourishing community, with pride in itself, the achievements of its members, and the obvious goodwill of all. There needs to be, and can be, a strongly expressed sense of the personal worth of each person, whoever she or he is (of course including support staff and visitors). The tutor can make a significant contribution to the overall climate or relationships in the school, but the tutor's work with the tutor group will be made harder if that overall climate is harsh.

However, within the group, tutors are well advised to establish a carefully controlled style which is efficient, fair, interested, positive and warm. From the mutual respect of member to member grows the wider respect for others. Personal and social development is best enhanced in the context of a tutor group which is a supportive 'group', and in a tutor room that is a true 'home room'. To achieve this for the group, then, each tutor will want to consider the following:

## The physical environment

To what extent can you make your room more pleasing, more welcoming, more stimulating? The ingenious tutor can use pin-boards, bookshelves, plants and pictures to soften and enliven the room, thus making it both more warm and more educative: the environment teaches.

## A spirit of fairness and caring

If members of the group are to develop as individuals, they must be helped to see that everything is done fairly and that each cares for each. Small touches, like the tutor's sending messages home about family events, sympathy offered to a boy who has lost something, or the group celebration of an individual's happiness, can build up a caring, group feeling.

### Group responsibility

As far as possible the group as a whole should discuss and make joint decisions of all kinds. In this way, also, the group can start to take responsibility for each other – helping the girl who is frequently late or the boy who often forgets.

### Build up a sense of achievement

Whenever possible, bring in work from the visual arts, the tutees' writing, their subject folders, and beyond-timetable events: praise them and display them.

## Working with uncertainty

Even the most knowledgeable and experienced subject teacher will find occasions when she is uncertain about the full facts, correct explanation or a proper way of presenting some aspect of a topic that arises. However, her or his teacherly stance is reasonably one of knowing most aspects of the curriculum that the pupil has to cover. This is not the case for the tutor. Indeed, even the most knowledgeable and experienced will know themselves to be ignorant of many topics that belong to personal and social development. Even when we have some knowledge, we are likely to be uncertain and know our limits. For instance, the development of understanding of HIV was so rapid that even a group of health education experts would disagree about some key details of transmission. Probably no teachers are going to be confidently knowledgeable, and most of us are going to know how little we know. For instance, a teacher was asked by girls in Year 10 whether women could pass HIV to other women. She had to say that she did not know. (Indeed, it proves to be less than clear: it is 'biologically plausible' that lesbian lovers could transmit HIV from vaginal fluids, but no cases have been recorded.) Similar ignorance is the frequent experience of tutors. It is an inevitable part of tutoring – as it is of parenting.

Further, it could be argued that lack of knowledge and lack of certainty are not only inevitable but desirable for the tutor over a range of his work. A subject teacher may reasonably hope to be happily confident over most of the course content. However, if the tutor's subject is the pupil himself, the tutor could not pretend to such major knowledge.

Perhaps one could think of the tutor's knowledge of the tutee and of life as a Venn diagram:

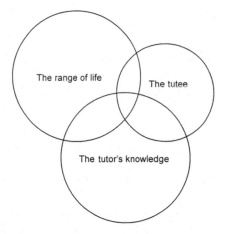

Figure 7    The intersection of tutoring

At the intersection of the tutor's knowledge with the other two circles is tutoring: but that tutoring has to pay respect to the unknown or only slightly known outer segments of the other circles. Such 'not knowing' is indeed a major mode of tutoring, and the tutor needs to feel confident with it, sharing uncertainty without being over tentative.

## The personal and the private

In handling many of the aspects of tutorial work tutors are faced with often difficult and subtle questions of how open or personal to be. On the one hand, the sensitive and conscientious tutor rightly fears being too 'distant' and impersonal, even cold, about those many topics which are essentially warm, personal and delicate. On the other hand, questions of tact, probity and reticence lead most of us to worry lest we should lay ourselves open to being hurt (perhaps by receiving mockery), being accused of pushing our own views, or prying into the lives of families. Many aspects of the curriculum involve controversial issues – literature, politics, the arts, even the apparent objectivity of the sciences. A school, a teaching team and each individual teacher has, of course, to develop a policy on the covering of contentious issues. The extended responsibility for the curriculum and management of the school since the major legislative changes of the late 1980s, the 1990s and 2002 (and despite the detailed requirements of the 2002 National Curriculum) has sharpened the need for a school to develop a policy. Such a policy both helps and protects individual teachers, while enabling them to develop further skills. Only with such an approach can pupils be brought positively to grapple intelligently for themselves with the powerful contentious issues of their lives.

Too many aspects of the years of secondary schooling are characterized by an emotional starvation. The tutor will want warmth, lightness, emotion and fun in the tutor room. She will want an atmosphere in which feelings, hopes, worries and joys can be shared, but will seek to achieve this without breaking an appropriate privacy.

One of the arts of the tutor is *to be personal without being private*. Many tutorial units would wither if there were not a personal tone, but the tutor should not confuse this with either revealing her or his own privacies or intruding into the tutees'. For a teacher to offer inappropriate intimacies about his private domain is in effect a challenge to the tutees' privacy because of the implicit expectation of reciprocation. Conversely, a tutor who offers details of his private personal life risks not only offending the tutee and her family but also prompting further probes, which could then offend the tutor.

## Towards good behaviour

There need be no tension between 'care' and 'control'. The disciplinary requirements of any school relate to the pastoral curriculum in such a way that respect for persons grows out of the whole-school pastoral curriculum, and especially the tutorial programme.

Behaviour can indeed be taught, and this is analogous to the worldwide use of the phrase 'reading recovery': just as those children who did not pick up aspects of reading which most do in early primary years can be helped by a later fresh, specific approach, so can those who missed out on the learning of inter-personal skills, self-esteem, and behaviour in childhood.

Specific behaviour skills' teaching is an aspect of every teacher's job, but it is the core of tutoring. This starts with encouraging attitudes. As one specialist has put it:

> The thrust of a truly personal and social education, of a school and a curriculum which is truly pastoral, will be to create conditions within which children will move as quickly and painlessly as possible to a position where they understand and cherish the values which the school should exist to promote: rationality, an open mind, a concern for the truth, respect for persons, and so on.
>
> (Best, 1988, p. 5)

The tutor's approach is the main way of enabling the pupils to 'understand and cherish the values'. How he or she handles the details from attendance to communications with home, from behavioural discussions to checking homework will bring the details of school injunctions to relate to the higher, longer-term ideals: explanations of why we need absolute quiet and immediate obedience in a fire drill; advice to the pupil who was rude to another teacher; a discussion of how to react to and make use of critical comments by a teacher on a piece of work. Every episode is handled not only for itself but also, with varied emphasis, as a lesson for the longer term.

In doing this we have to be careful not to confuse the agreed rules of convenience with deeper issues of ethics. Michael Rutter stresses the difference between 'house rules' and 'moral values' (Rutter, 1983, pp. 62–3 and 68–9), pointing out that they should not be confused: a school building, like every other community, will have practical regulations. These are to be followed for con-venience and order. As he says, 'It is important . . . that we do not create major moral issues where none exist' (ibid.).

The complementary converse of that is that where there are ethical issues, however small, they should be woven into the behaviour discussion. Even getting through a swing door in a crowded corridor has actions derived from ethical principles and illustrates them.

## The Form Tutor's example

In a slightly different but equally important way the tutees learn from the interactions with their tutor and her or his personal ways.

It is a truism of life that example teaches more than exhortation, and parents and teachers have always known that how they are to each other and to young people is an important component of educating young people. Adolescents say this themselves, and a research study of teenagers in this country confirmed that they felt little changed by advice on how to behave if those giving it did not themselves embody that advice in their ways of relating (McPhail et al., 1972).

It is striking how much a tutor can influence her tutees by the apparent intangibles of personality and her own inter-personal behaviour to other adults as well as to pupils. Michael Rutter helpfully focuses this in the following polarity:

> Sometimes we may wish that our children would 'do what we say', rather than 'do what we do' but it is clear that, when they clash, children tend to follow their precepts of our values, rather than our precepts of what they should practise. Children show a marked tendency to 'model' their behaviour on that of those whom they love, trust and respect.
>
> (Rutter, 1983, p. 69)

Our professional stance has always to be deliberately adult: our courtesy, sensitivity, vocal tone, humour and helpfulness are not only a management method, they are themselves a form of *teaching*. For instance, the pupil with her or his parent at a parents' evening will, perhaps unconsciously, be observing how her or his tutor reacts to the parent: any awkwardness, slight aggression, or lack of warmth will be an unhappy 'tutorial lesson' to that pupil.

## The atmosphere of tutoring

All aspects of teaching offer the problem of how objective or how personal the teacher should aim the discourse and interaction to be. Although there will be cool, even distant, sequences in tutoring, there need also be warmth, celebration and joy.

An American researcher said after his study of 1000 United States classrooms: 'There was remarkably little evidence of joy in learning . . . and the emotional tone was remarkably uniform' (Goodlad, 1984, p. 7).

While the discipline must be exemplary, the organization meticulous, and the curriculum planning for the tutorial programme rigorous, there has to be another dimension: the tutorial warmth. Of course, warmth, perhaps more professionally known as empathy, is an element of many successful lessons, and equally certainly the sloppiness that sometimes creeps in of 'pastoral care equals warmth' is incomplete and dangerous. There is nevertheless a real sense in which a heightened empathy is the essential *foundation* of pastoral care.

The tutor will always need to be rigorous in all respects, but without a patent warmth the tutorial group and its work will lack heart and conviction. The tension between generous warmth and objective judgement is the stuff of the tutorial atmosphere and the taxing balance of the tutor's special professional task. Indeed, necessary criticism and instructions are more effective when the tutee is secure in her or his experience of the tutor's warmth.

It is out of this feeling that the tutor will be able to counsel the occasional acceptance of difficulty and even unfairness: 'Yes, Mr Jones treated you unfairly, but sometimes life is just like that. There's really little we can do.' Conversely, it is out of such a warmth that there comes the flow of positive and generous spirit that encourages tutees to offer their titbits of information: 'He did really well in Art today; he got a commendation, Miss!'

The effective tutor will bed the work of the group into a warm soil, and out of it will grow trusting activities.

## Sharing with other Form Tutors

Generally speaking, tutor teams are, for a variety of reasons, less cohesive and less used to working together than subject course departments. The Year Head's team management role is in many ways harder than the Head of a Course Department's. The latter has usually played a part in the selection, appointment and induction of each member of the Department. The team very probably meet more often than a tutorial team can. Further, most will have the same subject degree and training, and thus share a greater intellectual engagement. Importantly, the Course Department team normally stays together, whereas fairly often tutorial teams are re grouped. There tends to be less 'lesson observation' of tutor by tutor, and even in many schools tutor by Year Head.

However, in devising aspects of the Tutorial Programme, in considering how to handle it, in sharing ideas about ways of working with tutees, tutors are immensely strengthened if they are helped to share ideas between themselves. Every tutor can learn a great deal from others: even the old hand can learn from observation or discussion with a new tutor. The challenge of this unusual tutee might be echoed by a tutee in a different group. In planning the whole-group work extra material may be desirable. One member of the team can devise it for this topic and another for a different topic. More than that, if tutors in a year come to sections of the tutorial programme in a staggered sequence, reactions, planning and ideas for approach can be shared, based on the experience of the first user.

Ideally, a team should build up sub-specialists, each of whom focuses on an aspect of the tutorial programme. Thus, one member might especially consider information-handling skills and study skills, another education in sexuality, and so on. In some cases this could develop virtually as team teaching, or team tutoring!, with some visits from other teachers to certain tutorial sessions so that strengths are utilized to the fullest.

Overall it is important to do as much as possible to contribute to the tutorial team, to help build it up as a complementary team, and to use its strengths. Tutoring can be a lonely business, though many team leaders work hard and successfully to avoid this. The tutor in a real team is stronger that the tutor alone.

# Conclusion

The work of the successful tutor will enable the students to take rational, morally sound, socially responsible, and personally deepening control over their lives in their culture and society. Ofsted has highlighted the core of schooling as 'spiritual, moral, social and cultural development', declaring: 'Most teachers would see it [SMSC] as the heart of what education is all about – helping pupils grow and develop as people.' (Ofsted, 2004) While every aspect of the whole school is responsible, the work of the form tutor has a very special responsibility.

The tutor's sensitivity and skill welds the routine and the special, using mechanical tasks like diary checklists to deepen self-aware-ness. The whole curriculum is served by and serves the tutorial programme. The study of how to understand and influence society appropriately relates to the tutee's growing sense of self and her or his responsibilities. The day is shaped by the tutorial framework and the habit of reflecting on their day becomes a cohering force for the tutees.

Thus the tutor's work substantially helps the tutee develop as a person into a growing adulthood. At the same time, in focusing on how best to make good use of the school the tutor is powerfully helping the 'child' develop into a 'student'. While a range of other forces is of course also very important, the tutor's contribution is special. Pupils are enabled to pull themselves up to greater school achievement not merely by the aggregate of good curriculum planning and teaching in the school's courses but also by the integrative work of tutoring.

The work of secondary-school tutoring is one of the most rewarding aspects of teaching. The form tutor is the integrative centre of the school. Her or his relating of the practical details of the day to the longer-term vision of adolescent growth of child into student and student into person can enable considerably greater academic and personal development.

# References

Allen, L. (1987) *Education in Sex and Personal Relationships*. London: Policy Studies Institute.

*Anti-social Behaviour Act* (2003) London: TSO.

Balding, J. (1987) 'Health Education', in Thacker *et al.*, pp. 172–9.

Belsky, J. and R. Isabella (1988) 'Material, infant and social-contextual determinants of attachment security', in J. Belsky and T. Nezworski (eds) *Clinical Implications of Attachment*. Hillsdale, NJ: Erlbaum.

Bennis, W. and P. W. Biederman (1997) *Organizing Genius: the secrets of creative collaboration*. London: Nicholas Brearley Publishing.

Best R. (1988) 'Care and Control – are we getting it right?' *Pastoral Care in Education* 6 (2) (June). Warwick: NAPCE: 2–9.

Botvin, G., A. Eng and C. Williams (1980) 'Preventing the Onset of Cigarette Smoking through Life Skills Training', in *Preventive Medicine* 9, 135–43.

Brecht, B. (1966) *The Exception and the Rule*, 1st UK edn in *Spotlight*, ed. M. Marland for schools. Glasgow: Blackie. First published in Moscow (1937) as *Die Ausnahme und die Regel*.

British Paediatric Association (1995) *The Health Needs of School Age Children*. London: BPA.

Bulman, L. and D. Jenkins (1988) *The Pastoral Curriculum*. Oxford: Basil Blackwell.

Button, L. (1987) 'Developmental group work as an approach to personal social and moral education', in Thacker *et al.*, pp. 130–43.

Charlton, A. and V. Blair (1989) 'Absence from school related to children's and parental smoking habits', in *British Medical Journal* 298 (January).

*Children Act* (1989) London: HMSO.

Cohn, D. A. (1990) 'Child–mother attachment of six-year-olds and social competence at school', *Child Development* 61, 152–62.

Committee of Enquiry (1985) *Education for All*, chaired by Lord Swann. London: HMSO.

Covington, M. B. and R. G. Beery (1976) *Self-Worth and School Learning*. New York: Holt, Rinehart & Winston.

Del Greco, L. (1980) 'Assertiveness training for adolescents: a potentially useful tool in the prevention of cigarette smoking', in *Health Education Journal* 39 (3) 80–3.

Department for Education and Employment (1994) *Code of Practice on the Identification and Assessment of Special Educational Needs*. London: HMSO.

Department for Education and Employment (1995a) *Protecting Children from Abuse: the Role of the Education Service*, Circular 10/95. London: DfEE.

Department for Education and Employment (1995b) *School Teachers' Review Body: Fourth Report 1995*. London: HMSO.

Department for Education and Employment (1997) *School Teachers' Review Body: Sixth Report 1997*. London: The Stationery Office.

Department for Education and Employment (1999) Circular 10/99. London: DfEE.

Department for Education and Employment (2000) *Sex and Relationship Education Guidance*, DfEE/0116/2000. London: DfEE.

Department for Education and Employment and The Qualification and Curriculum Authority (1999a) *The National Curriculum: Handbook for secondary teachers in England*. London: DfEE and QCA.

Department for Education and Employment and The Qualifications and Curriculum Authority (1999b) *Citizenship, the National Curriculum for England*. London: DfEE and QCA.

Department for Education and Skills (2001a) *Special Educational Needs: Code of Practice*, DfES/581/2001. London: DfES.

Department for Education and Skills (2001b) *The Education (Special Educational Needs) (England) (Consolidation) Regulations 2001*, DfES, No. 3455. London: DfES.

Department for Education and Skills (2003a) *School Teachers' Review Body: Twelfth Report 2003*. London: TSO.

Department for Education and Skills (2003b) *The National Agreement on Workload Reform: raising standards and tackling workload.* London: DfES.

Department for Education and Skills (2003c) *Disapplication of the National Curriculum (Revised),* DfES Guidance 0076. London: DfES.

Department for Education and Skills (2003) *Every Child Matters.* London: TSO.

Department for Education and Skills (2003) *Managing Pupil Mobility,* Guidance ref: 0780, London: DfES.

Department for Education and Skills (2004) *Every Child Matters: next steps.* London: DfES

Department of Education and Science (1989) *National Curriculum: from policy to practice.* London: DES.

Department of Education and Science/Welsh Office (1989) *Discipline in Schools.* Report of the committee of enquiry chaired by Lord Elton. London: HMSO.

Department of the Environment (1988) *The Local Government Acy 1989, Circular 12/88.* London: HMSO.

Department of Health (1996) *Child Health in the Community: a guide to good practice.* London: NHS Executive.

Department of Health/Department for Education and Skills (2000) *Guidance on Education of Children and Young People in Public Care.* London: DH/DfES.

Dweck, C. (1977) 'Learned helplessness and negative evaluation', in *Education:* 19 (2) (Winter). University of California and Graduate School of Education: 44–9.

*Education Act* (1993) London: HMSO.

*Education Act* (2002) London: TSO.

*Education Reform Act* (1988) London: HMSO.

Erikson, E. H. (1971) *Identity, Youth and Crisis.* London: Faber.

Explanatory Notes, *Education Act* (2002) London: TSO.

Gardner, H. (1983) *Frames of Mind: the theory of multiple intelligences.* London: Fontana.

Gardner, H. (2003) 'Multiple Intelligences after Twenty Years', paper presented at the American Educational Research Association, Chigago, 21 April 2003.

General Teaching Council for England (2002) *Teaching and Learning: the role of other adults.* London: GTCE.

Goleman, D. (1996) *Emotional Intelligence: why it can matter more than IQ*. London: Bloomsbury.

Goodlad, J. (1984) *A Place Called School*. New York: McGraw-Hill.

Hallam, S. (1996) *Improving School Attendance*. Oxford: Heinemann Educational Books.

Haselden, L. (2004) *Focus on Ethnicity and Identity*. London: Office for National Statistics.

Herbert, G. (1989) 'A whole-curriculum approach to bullying', in D. P. Tattum and D. A. Lane (eds) *Bullying in Schools*. Stoke-on-Trent: Trentham Books in association with the Professional Development Centre.

HMI (1982) *The New Teacher in School*. London: HMSO.

HMI (1987) *Quality in Schools: the initial training of teachers*. London: HMSO.

HMI (1988) *The New Teacher in School: a survey by HM Inspectors in England and Wales 1987*. London: HMSO.

HMI (1989) *Personal and Social Education from 5 to 16,* Curriculum Matters series 14. London: HMSO.

HMI (1993) *The New Teacher in School: a survey by HM Inspectors in England and Wales 1992*. London: HMSO.

Hodes, M. (2000) 'Psychologically Distressed Refugee Children in the United Kingdom', *Child Psychology and Psychiatry Review* 5 (2).

Howard, J. (1991) *Information Skills and the Secondary Curriculum*. British Library Research Report 84.

Kibble, D. G. (1988) 'Helping Parents through Exams', *Pastoral Care in Education* 6 (3) (September).

Kutnick, P. (1987) 'Autonomy: the nature of relationships, development and the role of the school', Thacker *et al.*, pp. 65–77.

Lees, J. and S. Plant (2000) *Passport: A Framework for Personal and Social Development*. London: Calouste Gulbenkian Foundation.

Lessing, D. (1965) *A Proper Marriage*. London: MacGibbon & Kee.

Lincoln, P. (1987) *The Learning School*. British Library Research Report 62.

Macbeth, A. (1989) *Involving Parents*. Oxford: Heinemann Educational Books.

McPhail, P., J. R. Ungoed-Thomas and H. Chapman (1972) *Moral Education in the Secondary School*. Harlow: Longman.

Maher, P. and R. Best (1984) *Training and Support for Pastoral Care.* Warwick: NAPCE.

Marland, M. (1980), 'The Pastoral Curriculum', in R. Best, C. Jarvis and P. Ribbins (eds) *Perspectives on Pastoral Care.* Oxford: Heinemann Educational Books.

Marland, M. (1981) *Information Skills in the Secondary Curriculum.* Schools Council Curriculum Bulletin 9. London: Methuen Educational.

Migration Research Unit, University College London (2000) *Pupil Mobility in Schools.* London: Nuffield Foundation.

Migration Research Unit, University College London (2004) *Pupil Mobility in Secondary Schools.* London: Nuffield Foundation.

Mosley, J. and M. Tew (1999) *Quality Circle Time in the Secondary School. A handbook of good practice.* London: David Fulton Publishers.

National Mentoring Network (2002) *Advice for Mentors Working in Schools.* London: NMN.

National Statistics (2004) *Focus on Ethnicity and Identity,* National Statistics, www.statistics.gov.uk/focuson/ethnicity.

Newsam, P. (1986) 'Racial Prejudice', *Association for Child Psychology and Psychiatry Newsletter* 8 (1) (January): 7–11.

North Westminster Community School (1991) *Aims.* London: NWCS.

Ofsted (1993) *Framework for the Inspection of Schools.* London: Ofsted.

Ofsted (1997) *The Annual Report of Her Majesty's Chief Inspector of Schools: Standards and Quality in Education 1995/96.* London: TSO.

Ofsted (1999) *Raising the achievement of minority ethnic pupils.* Ofsted Publications, ref: HMI 170. London: TSO.

Ofsted (2001) *The Induction of Newly Qualified Teachers: implementation of DfEE Circular 5/99,* HMI 270. London: Ofsted.

Ofsted (2004) *Promoting and evaluating pupils' spiritual, moral, social and cultural development,* HMI 2125. London: Ofsted.

Ofsted (2004) *Standards and Quality 2002/3: The Annual Report of Her Majesty's Chief Inspector of Schools.* London: TSO.

O'Shea, B., M. Hodes, G. Down and J. Bramley (2000) 'A School-Based Mental Health Service for Refugee Children', *Clinical Child Psychology and Psychiatry* 5 (2).

Pring, R. (1984) *Personal and Social Education in the Curriculum.* London: Hodder & Stoughton.

QCA (Qualifications and Curriculum Authority) (1997) *Spiritual, Moral, Social, and Cultural Educations*. London: QCA.

Robins, L. and M. Rutter (eds) (1990) *Straight and Devious Pathways from Childhood to Adulthood*. Cambridge: Cambridge University Press.

Rogers, R. (1994) *Teaching Information Skills: a review of the research and its impact on education*, British Library Research Series. London: Bowker Saur.

Rudduck, J. (1983) 'In-service courses for pupils as a basis for implementing curriculum change' in *British Journal of In-Service Education* 10 (1) (Autumn).

Rudduck, J., G. Wallace and S. Harris (1995) 'It's not that I haven't learnt much. It's just that I don't understand what I'm doing': metacognition and secondary-school students, *Research Papers in Education* 10 (2): 253–71.

Rutter, M. (1983) *A Measure of Our Values, Goals, and Dilemmas in the Upbringing of Children*. London: Quaker Home Service.

Rutter, M. (1989) 'Pathways from Childhood to Adult Life', *Journal of Child Psychology and Psychiatry* 30 (1): 23–51.

SCAA (Schools Curriculum and Assessment Authority) (1996) *Education for Adult Life: the spiritual and moral development for young people*, SCAA Discussion Papers No. 6. London: SCAA.

SCAA (Schools Curriculum and Assessment Authority) (1997) *Spiritual, Moral, Social, and Cultural Development*. London: SCAA.

Shah, M. (2001) *Working with Parents*. Oxford: Heinemann School Management.

Short, G. and B. Carrington (1991), 'Unfair Discrimination: teaching the principles to children of primary school age', *Journal of Moral Education* 20 (2).

Taylor, D. A. and P. L. Harris (1984) 'Knowledge of strategies for the expressions of emotion among normal and maladjusted boys: a research note', *Journal of Child Psychology and Psychiatry* 24 (1).

Teacher Training Agency (1997) *Standards for the Award of Qualified Teacher Status*. TTA.

Teacher Training Agency (2003a) *Qualifying to teach, Professional Standards for Qualified Teacher Status and Requirements for Initial Teacher Training*. TTA, TPU 1065.

Teacher Training Agency (2003b) *Qualifying to teach, Handbook of Guidance*. TTA, TPU 1064.

Thacker, J., R. Pring and D. Evans (1987) *Personal Social and Moral Education*. Windsor: NFER–Nelson.

Tomlinson, K. (2003) *Effective Interagency Working: a review of the literature and examples from practice*. LGA Research Report 40. Slough: NFER–Nelson.

Watkins, C., E. Carnell, C. Lodge, P. Wagner and C. Whalley (1998) *Learning about Learning*. Warwick: NAPCE.

Watts, M. (2003) 'Schools in White Areas', in *Race Equality Teaching* 22 (1). Stoke-on-Trent: Trentham Books.

Watts, M. (2003) 'The World Voices Project: Implications for Multicultural Interventions in Monocultural Schools', in *Race Equality Teaching* 22 (1). Stoke-on-Trent: Trentham Books.

Young Minds (1996) *Mental Health in Your School: a guide for teachers and others working in schools*. London: Jessica Kingsley Publishers.

# Helpful organizations

Although most tutorial consultations are made with specialist staff in your school or associated with your school through the LEA, the following national organizations are valuable for seeking specialist advice:

The National Association for Pastoral Care in Education (napce)
Education Department
University of Warwick
Coventry
CV4 7AL

Tel: (024) 765 23810    Fax: (024) 765 24110
Email: napce@napce.org.uk
(Many tutors find membership helpful and the *Journal* is very interesting.)

Connexions, a national organization with a large number of local branches 'intended to support the work of personal advisers in helping young people make a successful transition to adult and working life'.
Head Office: 7th Floor
Grosvenor House
125 High Street
Croydon
Surrey
CR0 9XP

Tel: (020) 8649 6400

The National Mentoring Network, which is very helpful supporting mentors and giving advice to mentors working in schools

First Floor
Charles House
Albert Street
Eccles
Manchester
M30 0PD

Tel: (0161) 787 8600   Fax: (0161) 787 8100

The DfES education website for teachers and school managers www.teachernet.gov.uk/ is a valuable source of information, advice, reports, good practice and contacts on the range of issues covered in this book.

# Index